Life Between Alarms

Additional books by author:

Firehouse Fraternity Oral History Series:
Volume I: Becoming a Firefighter
Volume III: Equipment
Volume IV: Responding
Volume V: Riots to Renaissance
Volume VI: Changing the NFD

The Newark Riots: A View from the Firehouse

An Eerie Silence: An Oral History of Newark
Firefighters at the WTC

Hervey's Boys: New Jersey's First Chinese Community
1870-1886 (And What Happened After That)

Fiction:
The Firebox Stalker
The Hand Life Dealt you
A-Zou: A Woman Living in Interesting Times

Children's Fiction:
A Hundred Battles (YA)
A Broken Glass (YA)
Balancing Act (Middle Grade)

The Firehouse Fraternity

An Oral History of the
Newark Fire Department

Volume II

Life Between Alarms

Neal Stoffers

Springfield and Hunterdon Publishing
Copyright 2008
www.newarkfireoralhistory.com

First Printing: 2008

ISBN: 978-1-970034-16-5

Springfield and Hunterdon Publishing
East Brunswick, NJ 08816-5852

Dedicated to past, present, and future generations of Newark firefighters, and especially to the 67 firefighters who made the ultimate sacrifice upholding their oath to protect the lives and property of Newark's citizens.

Contents

Acknowledgements

The credit for much of this book goes to the members of the Newark Fire Department who gave so generously of their time to take part in my oral history project. The hours of recorded conversations they contributed will help preserve the history of Newark's fire department and of Newark itself. A list of those interviewed appears at the end of the book. This is their story. I am honored to tell it.

Foreword

This book is one of six which recount the experiences of Newark firefighters. Beginning with the memories of a firefighter appointed in 1942, they tell the story of New Jersey's largest city and her fire department as seen through the eyes of the men manning her firehouses. I have attempted to group related subjects together to give the reader a true feel for various aspects of the fire service. The comments of the men I interviewed are presented in order of appointment date. This method is an attempt to give a better picture of the chronology of the dramatic changes which occurred in the city of Newark and the fire service in general.

The seeds of these books were unknowingly planted in a small firehouse on Springfield Avenue and Hunterdon Street. It was here as a young firefighter that I sat in the kitchen of Six Engine and listened to conversations between veteran firefighters, captains, and Deputy Chiefs about a city and fire department that existed in another time.

In June of 1991, I began an oral history project to preserve the memories of these men and the generations of firefighters who followed. The purpose of this project was to capture not only the words, but the texture of their experiences. What was a firefighting career like during this period in Newark and by extrapolation in America? Fire departments across the country have shared the experiences of the NFD in one way or another. Whether read by a professional firefighter from New York City or by a volunteer firefighter from a small rural community, the stories will be familiar. The fire service is a small world with a common purpose.

It is hoped what is recorded here will show both a bygone era and the evolution of the Newark Fire Department into its present form. If others outside the fire service walk away with a better understanding of the firefighters and the fire departments that protect them, my time over the past years will have been well spent.

Chapter One: Daily Routine

Fredette: (appointed 1942) The captain would say, "You're in charge of the cellar and the sidewalk. You take care of the boiler. You take care of the ashes. You take care of the garbage. You take care of everything on the outside of the building. I have men to take care of the windows and the apparatus."

When we worked the twenty-four straight they used to have a two hour meal trick. That was if you had enough men. I didn't have a car, so after I would go out and eat, I would walk around the neighborhood. I would look in the alley and see which one had a fire escape and where the hydrants were. I got to know the hydrants pretty good. I could tell you up and down Springfield Avenue where there was a fire escape in the alleyway.

Vetrini: (appointed 1946) You had your cup of coffee in the morning. Talked to the boys about what happened the night before. Read the paper. Everybody had a place to take care of. If you were the driver, you took care of the rig. If you had enough men, two fellows would go upstairs; one would stay downstairs cleaning the quarters. Naturally, as we got short on manpower, it worked out a little different, but still you had one or two men assigned upstairs and say two men taking care of the apparatus and the floor area and the kitchen area. Every Saturday we washed the windows.

The rig got washed at least once during your day shifts. Especially if you knew the rig was out at night. If the rig didn't go out, you didn't have to wash it, but any time it went out it got washed down. That was standard. Then, on Saturdays without fail you would be polishing the apparatus. The fellows would help the drivers polish the brass, take care of the apparatus. Years ago we used to have to service extinguishes. We had to have a big container of acid. That usually fell on the hose men. The driver didn't really have to do that.

The brass would be polished maybe on Saturday. You would go over the whole quarters; cleaning your sliding poles and the knobs on your doors. That had to be done. Now, if the captain came in and he thought something needed to be cleaned besides the schedule, you would do it.

Redden: (appointed 1947) Average day, you'd come in, sit down in the kitchen, have a cup of coffee, and talk generally about what went on. Tell a few lies here and there. Then the captain would come in at maybe eight-thirty, between eight-thirty and nine and say, "Okay, today is window day. Today is brass day." And of course the driver, the first driver, automatically he's out at the rig and he's going over the rig. Shining it up and doing what's necessary with the rig; checking the liquid levels and so forth. Some of the guys would go upstairs and do the bunkroom. Brush the floor and make sure all the beds are in good shape, dust it, do the bathrooms upstairs. If there was wet hose, you had to hang it.

There was a schedule. I don't remember what the schedule was, but everything was covered, windows, floors. Once a week you washed out the first floor, washed the floors. And of course outside, every day you'd sweep up outside. You could be done by ten, ten-thirty. Then your time was your own.

Kinnear: (appointed 1947) The average day, I don't think that's changed that much. You went in. You relieved your man; put your rubber coat at the time, helmet, and boots on the rig. Then went back into the kitchen and had a cup of coffee. Talked around the table and probably read the paper, no television of course, about eight-thirty, nine o'clock the captain would say

"Okay, let's go. Let's start cleaning up the place." One man would be assigned to the second floor. The other guys would clean up the first floor. The man on the watch, of course, always stayed downstairs. One of the other men would be assigned upstairs. The first driver would take care of the apparatus. We'd sweep the floors, once a week wet the floors completely. Back then all the wet hose had to be hung in the hose well.

You had your assigned days. Certain days were window days. Certain days you'd do the floor. Certain days take out the garbage. Of course, at that time we didn't have the luxury of automatic heat like you have today. We had a coal burning furnace and a pot stove for hot water. So you always had to run down the cellar and throw a few shovels of coal on the furnace. The pot stove, you had to make sure that didn't go out.

We had one captain. He was an older man, in his sixties, sixty-two when he made captain and they used to call him "iron beard." His one big thing was "Make sure that water is hot." He loved scolding water to shave with. So, when I was working with him, you made sure that stove stayed hot. Then there was taking out the ashes twice a week.

There was no "on the road" stuff like you do today, no in-service inspections or go to the store. We didn't do that with apparatus because you didn't have any radios on the apparatus. You had to be in quarters to receive the alarms. So, basically you were tied to the house. Twice a year they would send a guy out doing hydrant inspection. That would get stirred up. One guy would go out for two hours and he'd bring a can of grease with him and a wrench. He'd do the hydrants in a certain area.

About eleven-thirty, twelve o'clock one guy would go to the store; pick up the lunch for everybody. In those days on Springfield Avenue, you had four or five delis within walking distance. Or you had stores where you'd buy Italian hot dogs or things like that. Today that's changed. We had choices of stores. But basically, the day is the same except for the fact that now you can get out of the firehouse and do things. Building inspection was almost nil in those days. Very, very little building inspection was done.

Masters: (appointed 1947) Housecleaning, the first hour of the day was housecleaning. You had to make all your beds and we'd mop the bunk room. You check the apparatus for gas, check all your equipment. Then you get underneath. You drain that pet cock for the air brakes. We had to grease our own apparatus about every three months or so. Whichever tour was working, you greased that apparatus. You start from the back and you work forward, grease all the fittings. They did away with that. I guess the mechanics were complaining. We used to go down to Prospect Street and have the apparatus checked out. You had to wash the apparatus. If you came back in the rain you had to dry it, wipe it all.

The last man in took care of the furnace and the pot stove. We had a huge furnace, eighty tons of coal to shovel; take the ashes out. You'd polish the brass on brass day, the pole and the railing that went around the pole hole. The only bad feature about a clean pole was some guys weren't fully awake. They'd slide down the pole, hit that rubber mat, and end up with a broken ankle if they didn't hit it right. We'd leave them there. There's a fire. We'd call the operator. Send an ambulance up.

The captain would have us pull the apparatus out on the Ninth Street side and we'd drill every morning, a couple hours. It was nice. Then when I went over to the truck, we'd pull the truck alongside, raise the aerial, and run the hose through the ladder pipe. We kept busy. After that the day was yours. Work on the cars in the back yard, change the oil.

F. Grehl: (appointed 1948) It changes as you go through the ranks. As a firefighter, we had our housework to do. If you were in a company where they were ambitious, the captain had a small drill of some nature. When I was in Twenty-nine Engine and Ten Truck, the captain in the truck was my father. When he drilled the truck, Captain Schaffer made sure all the engine men went over and vis-a-versa. So, I had learned to raise an aerial even though I was never in a truck company.

That worked out because later on I spent quite a few months down in Five Truck as a temp in there. When the underwriters came to town, there I am in Five Truck. They come there and I'm sitting there with a Twenty-nine Engine front piece on. They asked, "What are you doing here?" I said, "I'm detailed here for the day." They said, "Okay, Cap. Take the apparatus out." We took the apparatus out. They said, "Okay, we're going to raise the aerial, but you raise the aerial." They pointed to me. So, the captain said, "He's not in the truck company. He's only detailed." "If he's detailed here today, he's supposed to do all the jobs of a truck man in this thing." Well, having been trained in everything, it was very simple. The aerial went up, beautiful. No problem at all. Of course, the captain was as happy as a lark.

Vesey: (appointed 1948) A certain day was brass day. Every day you cleaned up, mopped the bunkroom, do the toilets. All that stuff was daily. Brass was like twice a week and then windows. That took us a while. It all depended. Some places you had a bunch of slobs. In some joints, neatness counted. Not that they were carried away with it, but "Hey, I'm living here. I don't want to live in a shit house." Some guys couldn't care less. Thought they had maid service.

McCormack: (appointed 1949) Life in the firehouse was entirely different than it is today. You had a regular routine. There were certain rules you had to follow. It was mandated.

Masterson: (appointed 1949) It'd start out in the morning at the relief of tours. Both tours would be coming and going at the kitchen table with the coffee, talking. After that it would be almost nine o'clock, the Philadelphia firehouse lawyers would be arguing about different things. Then the housework would start according to what day it was. If it was Saturday we'd pull the apparatus out and clean the ladders. We cleaned the graphite. We'd scrub floors. Whatever had to be done, do the windows, we'd just do it. And we'd be doing it to about eleven o'clock because everybody worked, we'd shine the brass. There wasn't that large an amount of stuff to be done. In fact, no matter how hard you worked in Five Truck, it didn't look any better anyway.

I don't remember when they were, but there were brass days and window days. The brass I remember. That was the poles and I used them. When I left a lot of guys weren't using the poles anymore, but I used to always use the pole. If the pole wasn't clean, you'd stick on it. Cleaning it was for your own benefit. If you wanted to go down the pole, you'd clean it and shine it. We'd swab the whole apparatus floor out. When I first went on, the hose had to be dried. That was another part of the daily routine.

Ninety percent or more of the guys had all served in the war. They had all been in the service and back. They all had the same outlook on life. They all just came out of the Depression. That was the big thing, the Depression. The guys were all born in the '20s. You lived through the '30s and you went into the war. You came back and we thought we were doing great.

Deutch: (appointed 1953) We'd do our chores. In our particular case, the captain cleaned the kitchen and we all cleaned the rest of the firehouse and the apparatus. The tools we cleaned every day. The old timers were like that. If they came in and the tools were dirty, you cleaned and oiled them up. Radio came in right after I came on the job. So we could go out in the morning and do a few inspections in those days, too.

When I was at Thirty-five Engine, our day down there wasn't like up in the city. There was a sub-station for the Fifth Precinct with motorcycle stalls down there. There were only three of us riding on the truck. We just cleaned the firehouse and we were like an information station to Newark Airport. Everybody and his brother would come in and ask us how to get to the old, original airport building. Because the year I came on they opened a new one which is the North Terminal today. That was in '53. So, the airport wasn't flourishing in those days.

We took care of the apparatus; cleaned it every day. The chiefs were down, but we didn't drill as much down there as they did up in the city. I think the captains drilled us more. We used to go out and drill on abandoned buildings on our own, used all the ladders. I remember Johnny Fagan going out and we tried the pompier ladder. Stepped on it and it broke right off. The bottom step broke right off, the first rung. You had to climb one of them. We used them only on the abandoned buildings, never at a fire.

Wall: (appointed 1954) We actually had roll call, something probably that they wouldn't dare do today. You actually lined up and the officer saw you were standing, you had all your clothes on, and you weren't drunk. So we had roll call and an hour or so of housework. That brought you up someplace around lunchtime. If you had a straight line, serious officer, then you had a drill, at least an hour of drill in the afternoon. That was held either outside with the ladder if the weather was good or inside with the mask, whatever. We had a serious officer. Every day he had his hour of drill before anything else was done. Then after two o'clock, time was pretty much your own. If you were a serious person, you went and you did your studying for promotion.

You didn't go to the Academy much for in-service training as I recall. Maybe twice a year you went up and showed them you can throw a ground ladder or whatever. If there were some specialized thing that they wanted to bring out, something in fire prevention or something that was news, then they would bring companies up to Eighteenth Avenue. But you didn't have a drill ground.

McGee: (appointed 1956) In the morning, you'd come in; have your coffee; and a little conversation. They expected you to be on time, which we were, and you had a little bit of a roll call. In those days, you lined up even for the captain. After you had your line up, you were assigned whatever little duties, housework, and usually some sort of a drill if you had a captain who was interested in teaching you. I was fortunate that I did. After you did all that stuff, mostly in the morning, you would have lunch and the rest of the day was pretty much to yourself.

Some guys took that time to prepare for future promotion tests. Other guys found other activities to do. But it was pretty much left up to yourself after you completed what you were supposed to do. Then of course, you were always on the alert to alarms. Wednesdays were brass days and the brass got done, even the brass on the apparatus. Windows and cleaning outside quarters were other things we did religiously.

Stoffers: (appointed 1956) We went out on inspection; cleaned the brass on Saturdays. Our captain always did the ladders. On the engines, everybody worked different. Some guys would put the wet hose up in the hosewell to dry the first day they came in and other people would wait until four o'clock on their last day, in case they got a fire. That way they wouldn't have to go up there twice. It all depended on the individual companies.

McGrory: (appointed 1957) When I first came on, you went on inspections. You did your housework. You cleaned the rig. We had some sort of class. You had plenty of free time. The nights you didn't do too much unless you had a fire or there was something extra to do. You made sure the rigs were okay.

You had to do your work. You had time to yourself, if you wanted to study or do things. It wasn't as busy, but as the years went on it got busier. When I became a captain, I liked to do things, to go out. We used to drill and the fellows did a lot more. They cooked a little bit more. They didn't cook too much in Seventeen. When we changed captains, we used to have a big breakfast on Sunday morning. As time went on, I was promoted and my daily activity changed quite a bit.

Denvir: (appointed 1959) You had your cup of coffee and a roll or whatever. Probably around nine o'clock you'd start the housework. Then two guys would be upstairs, the other two guys would take care of the tools. The driver and the tiller man took care of the tools. If they were rusty, they would sand them down and oil them. Clean the axes and wash the truck. We would wash the windows in those days. The windows got washed. The brass got polished, all the brass. It would shine. You would work by the schedule you see in the firehouses. Some captains would come and check under the beds to see that everything was done. I always felt that when the guys who came home from the war got promoted to captain, they were more laid back. They had been through a lot and didn't get rattled.

Freda: (appointed 1959) Well, when I first came on the job, I happened to be assigned to a captain who became a captain later on in life. In fact, he was made a captain when he was in his fifties. He took the job very serious. He was still into some of the old school thinking of cleaning the apparatus after each run, especially if you went out in the rain. You'd have to come back and wipe the water off the rig. The house was always kept spotless. If the schedule called for brass to be cleaned on Wednesday, you would clean the brass on Wednesday. If Friday were window day, you would clean windows. And you would drill every day. He was more or less a man who ran things by the book. He didn't deviate too much from the book.

Charpentier: (appointed 1959) At the time I was appointed, both tours stood roll call at eight in the morning and six at night and then the tour going off duty left. You had to have the uniforms on at roll call. That only lasted about a year. Then later on as your relief came in you left, whether it was four o'clock in the afternoon, five o'clock, as long as it was before six. Mornings you'd come in. Eight o'clock you stood your roll call and between eight and eight-thirty you had your second cup of coffee, then you started.

The driver took care of the apparatus. You had to do your sweeping, your mopping. Certain days were for doing brass work. Certain days were for doing windows. The apparatus driver used to wash the apparatus at least one of the two days. He checked all his fuel, his oils, water, and the tire pressure. The other fellows just had their routine work to do, but it was a schedule that you followed.

Carragher: (appointed 1960) When I went to Rescue, Frank Combel was my captain. I worked with Barney Fabo and Johnny Coxton and Artie Knispel on the First Tour. Captain Combel was deep into training. Every day we had to train. Every day a different compartment on the apparatus had to be emptied out. If it looked a little marred or scratched, we painted the compartment, took care of the tools, and put them back in the compartment. Every day that we worked, we did a different compartment and worked around the rig.

When I went to Twenty Engine, it was like night and day. We didn't have compartments anymore. We didn't sweep too much anymore. We had an annual inspection and Chief Redden was the inspecting officer that day. When I got to the firehouse that day I said to a couple of the guys, "The inspection is at ten o'clock this morning." "Yes, okay. Let's have our coffee. We'll start cleaning up at nine o'clock." I said, "Yes, but the chief is coming around." He says, "That's all right. We'll start at nine. We'll be ready." So, we swept the floor, put the garbage out. The Chief came and said the house looks nice and walked out.

I had another good incident that happened at Twenty Engine. Dick Maiser was the new captain in Twenty Engine. He walked in around seven-thirty and introduced himself. We're shaking hands and talking. I was still in the Rescue Squad. Our crew was all there. We're talking to him and the guys from Twenty Engine are there and we're talking, coffee and everything. At eight o'clock Dick Maiser says, "Okay, who's my crew now?" And one of us says to him, "Well, Dick, none of your crew is in yet. They don't come in until about ten after, quarter after eight. No one is in yet." Well, he didn't know what to do, but he had to go along with it because the crew in Twenty Engine, everybody covered for everybody.

Haran: (appointed 1961) In Salvage we'd go in in the morning at the start of tour, you'd have your coffee. There were a lot of fires back then. We used to throw a lot of salvage covers. If there was a fire today, the tour coming in tomorrow used to go over to that fire scene and gather the covers when the water stopped dripping and coming down from the fire floor.

In the back of our quarters, in the Special Services building, there was a washroom. We had these big poles going across the ceiling. We'd drape the salvage covers over the poles and hang them up there. Then we had this high-pressure hose in there. We'd wash the salvage covers down with soap and water with heavy brushes and rinse them off with the hoses. Salvage Two used to come down from Belmont Avenue and we used to wash these salvage covers jointly on our second day in. They'd hang for two days and then whatever tour worked that day would take them down and fold them. We had a special way of folding them so that they would open up in a way that we could walk in opposite directions and the cover would open up. Then it would be in position to throw it over the furniture.

Every day we checked our equipment. We were a secondary rescue squad. We had acetylene apparatus on the truck. We had E & J oxygen cylinders which looked like the old footlockers in the army, but then they were big tanks. They were worked in conjunction with aspirators. We worked with that. We used to do first aid training. So, our day was pretty full. Most of the guys there were volunteers. They were interested in the job. Our day was pretty much training.

Cahill: (appointed 1963) The first thing you did was housework. You did housework on a routine basis. Saturday I think was brass day. Wednesday would be window day and you did it. As the pace increased throughout the department, that slowly faded away to the point where you just got down to the bathroom was clean and the living conditions were bearable. There was a strict routine that everybody adhered to. As it is today, there was always one tour that didn't do everything they were supposed to do. That was a beef. Which is the same as it is today. So, that hasn't changed.

You washed the apparatus, checked the masks. That was the first thing you did when you came in, religiously. We never had to wash the rig coming back from a fire. I heard old timers say that whenever they came back, even in the middle of the night, they would put the thing out there and wash it. If it was raining when they came back, they would pull it in quarters and wipe it off even if it was three o'clock in the morning. If you're going out ten minutes later, then you pull it back in and wipe it off again. I never witnessed it, but I've been told that that's what they did. I guess each generation has gotten a little more lax. But that's what it was, you had a routine and everybody did it. The new guys did the stuff nobody else wanted to do like climb the hosewell and go to the store for lunch. It wasn't really harassment. It was just something that everybody did. That was part of the job.

Highsmith: (appointed 1963) My average day in Nineteen Engine, we'd come in during the day. We'd have our coffee or breakfast or whatever. Then the two guys who drove, which would be me and Freddy Scalara, would take our turns in cleaning up, whether it was upstairs or downstairs. Jimmy Trimble and Jimmy Conlin would take care of the other and we'd do our cleaning for about an hour or so. After that it was lounge around time or we'd go out. We'd do some inspections, have lunch, and then after lunch it was waiting for the bells to hit until it was time to go home. But at the time it was real nice because I worked with a bunch of nice guys. They didn't mind pitching in, helping. Our firehouse wasn't in the best of shape, but it was always clean. Like I said, we were like a family down there in Nineteen Engine.

I think Wednesday was brass day. We had window days. I'm not too sure what that was at the time. Saturday was clean the apparatus day. That was always done. You always kept them shiny and clean and the equipment was always looked after.

Wargo: (appointed 1964) When I first came on things were a bit more military. You would do the housework every day. There was no thought of not doing it. Wednesdays and Saturdays were brass. I forget if it was Saturdays were windows, but those days you did those things. We did have drills and at that time the chiefs used to call you, take you down to the docks, down at the port and drill. Kept you going.

Garrity: (appointed 1964) The average day was breakfast every morning when we came in. Always did housework, that's the one thing Tommy Boil insisted on. We cleaned the firehouse, polished the brass when it was supposed to be done, washed the windows, washed the rig, cleaned the tools, and hung the hose. All that stuff had to be done before we did anything else. Once that was done, we were basically on our own to do whatever you wanted to do around the firehouse. We drilled every day. It was either sitting around the table or in nice weather we'd go out. Put the aerial ladder up, raise a few ground ladders and just basically fool around with the apparatus, things like that. Afternoon was naptime.

McGovern: (appointed 1968) Twenty-seven Engine at the time, the captain I had was Leo Jennings. Who was a retired Coast Guard Warrant Officer. Things were done the right way or not at all. The deal was nine o'clock housework started. Wednesdays you did brass. Thursdays you did windows. That's the way it was. I never minded it. The rule of thumb down there was if one guy works, everybody works. Instead of this one guy's doing all the work and the other three are reading the paper. If one guy got up to work, everybody worked. That's the way I was broken in. I think it's a good way to run a company. Routine, you knew what to expect.

D.Prachar: (appointed 1968) When I first came on, being the junior man, I probably didn't get to read the newspaper until I went home because the captain read it first and then the senior man. However they wanted to do it. Some houses they would bust your chops. First two days in the firehouse, like I said, I never saw the newspaper. I love to read my newspaper. Drill, out to drill. We had a coal furnace. It was my job the first couple of days to learn how to shovel coal, which I knew how to do, but nobody else in the house was going to do it because they were senior men and I was junior man.

You do your basic housework, apparatus, simonize. If it was your month to simonize the rig, you better make sure you simonize it. You had to simonize it because they wanted it shiny when it pulled out. If you had a spare, it didn't matter. That got simonized. Then when your own piece came back, that better be simonized, too. So you always wanted to make sure it wasn't your month to simonize or wax the rig.

You might go out to abandoned buildings and drill, but you didn't have many abandoned buildings then. Find a building to throw the aerial up to learn. My thing was I always wanted to tiller. I always used to see the man driving down the street. I wanted to be the man who drives the back of that fire truck. That was my thing. I always wanted to go to a truck company when I came on, basically for that reason believe it or not. Then when I learned how to tiller, I wanted to learn how to drive. That's when I went to Nine Truck. Right after I went to Nine Truck, Vinnie Mulvaney went to Nine Truck. Vinnie was like me. He came from an engine company. He wanted to learn how to tiller. I wanted to learn how drive. Richie Bitter was our captain and we told him, "Well, if Pat Bresslen or Bill Fink were out, one of us would have to drive. One of us would have to tiller." So, we finally annoyed Bitter enough that he took us out driver training.

Gerard Place is off Clinton Avenue. They have a little diamond park up in there. We tillered and drove around that park two and a half hours, backwards. Bitter said, "You wanted to learn. This is how you learn." Drove forward for a little bit to get our coordination and then drove backwards around that. People in the neighborhood thought we were crazy. Went back to the firehouse and then about a month later Bill Fink was on vacation and Pat was on sick leave, so we had to drive and tiller. Low and behold we hit the door going out. Apparently, going around that little park didn't help us going in and out of doors. Needless to say, Bitter was fit to be tied.

Cosby: (appointed 1969) First thing we did when we came in was the housework. After the housework, we would more or less go out and do inspections. That occurred around, maybe nine-thirty, ten o'clock in the morning. What we would try to do is target the hazardous buildings. Inspect those buildings. Find out what was in these buildings and how we would fight fires in them. After the inspections were done, then we would come back to quarters. Sometimes we would have training, but then after that we would just "wait for the big one."

Pianka: (appointed 1970) The routine hasn't changed that much from house to house, surprisingly. Breakfast, the usual coffee table banter and all the nonsense that we all think we know so much about which we really don't. We just express our opinions. Do the usual housework in the morning, so by ten o'clock you're essentially done as far as any mandatory work. You might have a drill scheduled or you have to run out of the firehouse to do something, which brought you right up to lunchtime because you started talking about lunch right after you had breakfast. That was our next goal in life, eating lunch.

Then in the afternoon we took our nap. Now if there were no fires that was it. It's a quiet, uneventful, boring life. Except for some fellows, some fellows were constructive. I remember Frankie Mastroeni was always doing something. If I had spare time, I'd go upstairs and read. That was my whole thing. I remember Elton Fisher used to do dental work. He was in the Air Force I believe and he was trained as a dental technician. I don't think as a modern day tech, but he could make up a set of teeth. He knew how to make plates or he knew how to get the impressions. I think he sent it away. People would come. He'd take them into the bathroom, sit them down on the toilet there, and he'd take the molds. That's how people were getting dental care. They were coming to Doctor Elton Fisher. Elton was a great guy.

McDonnell: (appointed 1970) They stuck to that schedule a lot. The discipline was a lot better. We did the brass on Saturday. Friday was window day. That might not get done all the time, but we washed the windows at least once a month. We did the brass every Saturday. The floors got mopped, I don't remember exactly, but Mondays and Wednesdays. You did upstairs. The general housekeeping, sweeping the floor and that sort of thing got done every day. You did what you were supposed to do. The rig got cleaned a lot more. You're supposed to come in and wash the rig. Guys did come in and wash the rig first day. The driver would wash the rig every first day that we worked. We did stick pretty much to that schedule. It was a housework schedule and it was stuck to.

Rotonda: (appointed 1970) Most of the time I made breakfast. Lenny Fondetta, only time he said anything is "What's for breakfast?" Anyway, I used to make breakfast all the time, until Lenny Fondetta retired. Then it started going down because now you're getting guys who are so one way. The only people they are interested in are themselves. You can't deal with people like that. So I would do my job, but I didn't do any extras. I was in the Army. If you tell me you want a bolt or you want your glass to be put on top of the TV, I'll put it on top of the TV. I know it belongs in the cupboard, but I won't put it in the cupboard. I'll put it on top of the TV. You want it on the TV? That's where you get it. I'm not going to help you until you discover it's in the wrong place. Then you have to come back again and do it. I know how they do it in the Army and I know how to survive the Army. I can survive because that's my nature.

Melodick: (appointed 1970) First of all everybody went to the table. We had our cup of coffee. Talked about probably what we did that day; who was doing a job for somebody; who in their family had a birthday; what they did on their days off; or whatever. We'd sit down and maybe we'd be watching the news or we'd be talking about something.

We had a Deputy, Chief Dolon. He was a great guy. Dressed right to a tee, perfect, everything pleated, shoes shined; the whole nine yards. What he expected was you go to a fire and do your job, but you did have housework. We had brass poles and religiously, they had to be cleaned. Avon Avenue was a pain in the ass if you were upstairs. It seemed like there were so many steps going up and down on Avon Avenue. We used to take the poles from the bunkroom down to the apparatus floor, which was great. When the chief came in the firehouse, he wanted the brass poles cleaned. Windows we did.

We had a ping-pong table. We used to play ping-pong quite often on Avon Avenue. Then in the back they had a basketball hoop and we used to go throw some baskets back there. We would do things between alarms. Watch TV; talk about our family life; joke around; play cards, or whatever else. They had a pool table, too. Guys would hang out down in the basement at the pool table. We had a radio in case of an alarm. One guy would have to stay upstairs. If we were going, he just let us know, "Hey, we're going." We had a lot of exercise because you were constantly going up and down the stairs. But everybody loved it. Nobody ever complained about that.

T. Grehl: (appointed 1971) Average day, you walked in, you just basically sat around the kitchen, had a cup of coffee, talked with the out going tour. First of all you put your gear right on the rig and you had to check the mask that you were going to use. Even though it's more advanced today, you still have the same basic principle. Because you weren't assigned your own face piece then, you always had to make sure that it was clean. It was a shared thing. The drivers used to check the fire engine at seven-thirty, when you walked in and you relieved a guy.

There was a lot more discipline then. People were actually afraid of some of their captains. We were afraid that the senior man might say, "Hey kid, did you check your mask?" "Ah, yes." But you might not have. There was a little fear. There was a little more discipline.

At nine o'clock without fail, housework started. Then after that there were actual inspections and drills, especially with myself when I first came on. Lardiere would drill me. I'll never forget. Because I was in a truck company, he asked, "Are you afraid of heights?" I said, "No, I'm not afraid of heights at all. I respect them. If you want to put me a hundred feet in the air, I respect them. But I'm not afraid of them." So he had me climb up and down the ladder outside the firehouse constantly. Whenever the driver took the rig out, he'd raise it to make sure the aerial worked that day. I'd go up to the roof. Took me down to the Hilton, I believe it was the Hilton, down around the airport. I guess it was sixty or seventy feet to the roof, raise the thing, go up there, and check the roof. I knew it was his way of testing to see if I would go up the aerial. There are different ways. Because we didn't have the Academy training to have certified teachers say, "Yes, he did." I guess he had to find out and that was his way. They handled it nicely.

We did do a lot of drilling in the beginning. They showed me a lot. Then after lunch, your time was free. Before I went to the Academy, he did make me look at a book or two. He'd sit down and go over various things with me. The afternoon was kind of your free time. At night we played cards, especially on the weekends. God bless his soul, but Captain Lardiere would never suggest it. He was so superstitious. He loved cards more than anybody, but he would never say, "Okay, let's play cards." Because he figured he would lose. He would never start the game. He would always say, "Yes." "Do you want to?" "Okay." But he would never say, "Are we going to play tonight?"

There was brass day. Saturdays I believe was windows. Don't remember when brass day was, but Brasso was used a lot. We used Brasso all the time, because the poles were all used. Not only did you have to do the poles, you had to do all the doorknobs, the doorknobs were all brass in the firehouse. We've become a little lax in the housework of today. Then it was an ordeal. You mopped all the floors every day. You made the beds. If a guy left his bed unmade from the night before, you had to fold the blankets on the bed, real neat. All the blankets had to be neat and tucked, so if anybody walked in it was presentable. The fire engine was washed every other day, like your first day in.

When I first went there it was a two piece company. They had the regular pumper and the wagon, they called it, which brought extra hose to the fire. So, actually they rode one and four. When they were down to one and three they just didn't use the wagon. They just manned the pumper. But the rookie had to go up the hosewell. Even though I was in the truck, I had to go up and hang the hose.

Ryan: (appointed 1973) The average day, brass and window days were part of our regular schedule. The captain would come down and tell us, "Today is windows day and Wednesday is brass day." We would do that. It was just part of our normal routine in the firehouse. That way everything was maintained very well. It was no great chore on any one tour. So, if you had a job or had an inspection or whatever you had to do and hadn't finished your daily work, you'd come back and do it.

Langenbach: (appointed 1973) We had Captain Cassidy. For Belmont Avenue, Cassidy was pretty strict about housework, nine o'clock we do our housework. And we'd always go out and do some kind of a drill. Either in the house or we'd go somewhere and do something. We always did inspections one of the two days, but the rest of the time was just fun and games.

Brass day was Saturday maybe. Windows was one day. Yes, as much as an upholstered toilet as Belmont Avenue was, it was still kept clean. The poles were shined up; the windows were washed. We did all those stupid things. Even though the cellar was full of the backed up sewage, it was still done. Stuff was still cleaned up. The truck every quarter belonged to one tour so it'd get washed and waxed with the DuPont number seven, the liquid wax. There was still a lot of respect for the job. No matter where you worked or how busy you were or whatever, it was still these things had to be done. Come back from a fire, you'd take the K-12 blade off and soak it in Varsol, put a new one on. Everybody checked the tools, cleaned the tools and everything like that. It was an interesting time.

Luxton: (appointed 1973) I always got in early. I always came in seven o'clock, six-thirty or seven, someplace in there, have a couple of cups of coffee. The captain would come out and say we're going to train on this or train on that. Chief McGrory was always one for having multi-company drills. We'd go out and drill with a deck gun or whatever. Sometimes it was drilling, but you learned a lot of it out on the street. Anytime I ever worked at Six Engine, day or night, we always went out. There was never a time we didn't respond to something. Maybe it was only one or two runs, but you always had something. There was never a time when I didn't go someplace.

Connell: (appointed 1974) It depends what you were assigned to do. You usually came in in the morning, had coffee, and talked with the tour going off duty. Just bullshitted, read the paper, TV whatever the case might be until nine o'clock. From nine to ten o'clock if you were the driver you had to go check the apparatus out, clean all the equipment, all the stuff. If you weren't assigned to driving the apparatus, your job was either upstairs or downstairs cleaning including washing all the bathrooms, sweeping and washing the bunkroom floor, dusting, polishing brass, washing windows. Windows if I remember right were Saturdays. Brass was Wednesdays. The day was yours after the housework was done except your first day in. You went out for two hours every day. You did in-service inspections. I was starting to study already, so a large portion of my day would be reading books, studying to improve my knowledge of fire.

Pignato: (appointed 1974) Most of the time you came in the first day, you had to clean. You usually cleaned for a couple of the other tours that didn't do their share. You cleaned the rig. You checked the rig. I was broken in on the rig right away by an old fireman, Anthony Masters. He used to get a creeper, climb under the rig with a rag and Varsol and wipe down the whole rig. It would look brand new. Of course, there should have been a person like this on every tour then the rig would probably be in better shape, but it wasn't. There were some tours that take care of things, some tours that didn't. That's what your life is in the firehouse, compromise. Some guys, their whole job is to just be firemen. They actually said, "We don't do housework. We don't clean toilets." We took care of the firehouse.

Our firehouse didn't seem to follow the rules. When I was detailed down to Three Truck/Seven Engine, they had a schedule and almost all the tours followed that schedule. The brass was shined beautiful down there and they did the windows. They did everything they were supposed to do. In my firehouse they didn't. One shift could do it. They were doing everybody else's work. It gets old real fast after a while. You start concentrating on the important things. You clean where you eat. You clean the toilet and you clean where you sleep. The rest of the place can go to hell.

Langevin: (appointed 1974) Your roll call is taken. Your captain would assign you a job and go over your equipment, make sure everything is there, start the saws. Then you do housework. The brass, all the brass in the firehouse was shined twice a week. Windows were done and that's in addition to the regular housework that's done every day. Like cleaning floors, cleaning the kitchen, cleaning the bathrooms, the shower areas, things like that. It took about an hour, hour and a half. After the housework you might drill or go out on inspection. This would take you up until lunchtime. After lunch you might have a lecture.

The other thing that was done that doesn't need to be done nowadays was hanging hose. The first thing that was done every morning, it didn't matter whether you were on a ladder company or an engine company, you hung hose in the hose tower. That was the first thing you did every morning. After that your time was your own. Interspersed in there the bell would always hit.

Perdon: (appointed 1974) When I first came on, I was at Four Truck which was slow. There were a bunch of young guys with me. Donny Hayes was there. He came on as a cadet, so he was brand new. Stanley Ford was there. We went from doing housework to wiffle ball to ping-pong. You had the basketball court right out there. We played basketball. We had Chief White. He was straight as an arrow. His idea of a party was hot cocoa and pumpkin pie. He saw what was going on and he wanted to make sure we took the job serious, so he put myself and Jimmy Jennings on the book for a month to make sure we knew the job isn't all games.

Actually I was just following the guys who were there. They would play wiffle ball. They would play ping-pong. And I just fell in line. We went a whole year between jobs. I caught a couple first on. They were decent jobs. Not the way they were fought, but guys up on the hill would have had a great time. We used to pray for move ups, pray for them, because that was our only shot at catching jobs. I lasted down there about a year, a little over a year, because I got to Seventeen Engine after the lay-offs.

We did brass and windows. You had to do them. Even when I got to Six Engine, we were doing that. You had these certain days; today was brass day, the other day was windows. Yes, we had to do the poles and had to clean the windows.

Lining up for the chief wasn't really big. They would be hot and cold on that. Even now it will become an issue for a little while and then it just goes by the wayside. They used to hit the gong. I was always in a Chief's house. Somehow I was always in a Chief's house. Very rarely I had to spend time with like Ten Engine. You're looking at close to thirty years. Maybe two years, well a little bit longer. Seventeen Engine, I'm forgetting that. But other than that, yes you used to hear the gong when the chief rolled in.

Bisogna: (appointed 1974) Coffee, read the paper, and back then we were busy so you had a little more to do as far as you made sure you got your stuff ready on the rig. I mean there was definite fire department business taken care of. We went on inspections. We actually went out the door and went door to door and said we're here for your complimentary fire department inspection if you like. Joe Hopkins was my captain. That guy was super. He was a "man among men" as they say. He was straight.

You did the fire department then you fooled around. Then we'd cook lunch. We went out and got lunch. As the Tact Squad we had the roam of the city, so we went anywhere we wanted to, got whatever we wanted to. Guys got to go "shopping." They'd go looking into abandoned buildings for thrown away antique stoves or anything they could scrounge. This stuff was all abandoned. It wasn't like you were stealing. I thought it was good because I got to see old homes that I would have never seen that are gone now.

Twenty Engine had a handball court right behind the kitchen. It had a little backyard that was walled in. They put a fence over it. The wall must have been fifteen feet high. It was a pretty solid brick wall with just a doorway in it with a basketball court, but you could play handball off the back wall and the two side walls. We did a lot of that. They played basketball, too, but I remember handball a lot. At night you'd play cards and backgammon. We'd play cards for a change.

I remember rumors of brass days and window days. Monday was windows, Tuesdays might have been brass. There definitely were. Whether we did it or not? That was another story. Nobody who I ever worked for was a real stickler for that, but you don't want to live in crap. You came in and nine o'clock, ten o'clock everybody would get up and just sort of mill around and clean up whatever, the toilets, and sweep up and once a month they would take a hose to the inside of the room because whatever needed to be done got done. They'd bleach the floors. They'd clean the kitchen pretty good. Always cleaned up after ourselves, but in most places that get along that's what happens. You don't really have to say it's time for housework, but it got done. Then inspections, whenever there was an inspection, you'd try to put on a little show for the Chief. Show him that you weren't screwing around.

We went to a lot of fires too. Most of the time they worried more about putting fires out than keeping things clean. Chiefs always looked the other way when it came to housework. But for the most part, you try to keep it sanitary at least. There weren't cobwebs hanging from the ceiling or anything. You did the best you can do in the city of Newark. They didn't come in and paint every ten years, so you lived with what you've got.

Ricca: (appointed 1974) Brass day, I believe brass day was Saturday and window day was Wednesday. Captain Titcomb was by the book. Brass day was brass day. Window day was window day. The rig was scrubbed, not cleaned, not washed, it was scrubbed. Brass day wasn't only the poles, but the locker knobs, the door knobs, the switch covers; anything that was brass was Noxoned on that day. The way it worked was that the engine had the first six months of the first floor and the truck had the first six months of the second and then they swapped. The captain touched nothing. The captain's room sink was cleaned. The room was dusted, mopped, whatever it need be. You didn't have the captains getting up and saying, "Let's start housework." The senior man would stand up nine o'clock, grab a broom and everybody would just follow behind him.

After I went to Five Truck, it would take nothing, coming back from a fire after a bad night with a bunch of runs, it would be nothing for Frankie Calvatti to say, "Ladder that building." It would of course be a vacant building, but it was a way that he kept us sharp. It almost became a second sense. You could raise the aerial with your eyes closed. It became part of you. When I was first taught I was in awe of Kenny Miller raising it and rotating it at the same time and extending it and lowering it until I got proficient at it and was able to do it. Then it became a show once again like everything, how fast, how quick, how many wires could you miss. Did you take down the telephone service to somebody's building?

Gesualdo: (appointed 1977) From the beginning, the average day was try to get in an hour early. That was kind of like an unwritten rule. You got in an hour early because guys wanted to get out and didn't want to get stuck at a last minute job and they usually reciprocated. In the evening, they'd come in an hour early for you. I guess it had something to do with the rush hour. If they would have left at eight o'clock the traffic would have been worse. I know for the morning shifts, I had to be on the road by a certain time to be here by seven. I was still living in Newark at the time, but about a year after that I moved out. I know that I definitely had to leave earlier to get here by seven o'clock. And the guys appreciated it. There was definitely a lot more friction back then about early reliefs than there is now. Now it's just accepted, guys just aren't going to come in early most of the time, but back then, especially when you were new, you got in at seven o'clock in the morning and five o'clock at night.

The day consisted of having your coffee in the morning, a little chat at the table. Eight o'clock apparatus check, bleed the air brakes; wash the rig. When you were new you kind of knew you were expected to do all that. I had no problem with that, kind of enjoyed it. It was a steady job. You have to work nights and part time jobs too much, but it was ten hour days and ten hours just seemed to usually fly by. We'd respond usually six maybe seven times a day. You had your lunch. At that time I think we had George Odell. George was kind of our cook and he would get lunch ready. Sometimes it meant leaving him behind if we were going out on building inspection or hydrant inspection. So, you got some perks when you were a chef. But I remember it being real interesting, a lot of busting, a lot of critiquing jobs when we got back.

We had window days on the work schedule around the firehouse, yes. Oh, yes. Brasso days, window days, waxing the apparatus days, yes. I remember there being a schedule there. We used to have to do all the brass, the poles, and then the windows. It didn't last too long. I would say maybe two, three years after I came on. It wasn't such a big issue to us after that. I remember we used to have regimented work, housecleaning. The brass didn't always get done on the day it was supposed to, the windows didn't always get done. It depended on which tour was working. I remember the fourth tour always being one of the conscientious tours, not slackers. You had some guys who didn't mind sweeping. You had other guys who didn't mind doing windows and everybody found their own little thing, they're own little specialty and they did it. If extra work had to be done because somebody was out on personal days or sick days, the work got picked up. Nobody seemed to complain about it and that was when you had more fires.

Chapter Two: The House-watch

Vetrini: Sixteen Engine had journals that gave you the history of taking care of the horses. They wrote down whose turn it was to clean the horse; to get the horse up in the morning. You had to get up at five-thirty in the morning or something, groom the horse and clean the stable. Truck Eight, the kitchen they have now was the stable and upstairs from there was the hay loft. Still, that is the structure of their building. Sixteen was built by the W.P.A. around 1932. They were originally located down Ferry Street down by Manufacture Place, facing Manufacture Place. When the building was done by the WPA, that is the Work Projects Administration during the Depression, they moved into their quarters where they are now. And if you will notice there are only three walls there. What they did was they used Eight Truck's wall and just faced it the ceramic brick on that side.

Redden: The house watch of course rotated to everybody. So, you were responsible for the book. You were responsible for anybody who was coming into the firehouse, possibly people looking for directions, and booking the alarms that came in. The time it came in, the box number, the location, and then when it was under control you book in the time. You're booking companies out and you're booking them in. We had a board with twenty-five engines and twelve trucks. So you knew what kind of condition the city was in.

Of course, if you had a run the captain would write in the book what was done. One of the things that I liked about driving the chief was I didn't have to do the book watch anymore. It was a long night. Some guys could sleep when they were on book watch, but I couldn't. I would sit in the chair. Nod off once in a while, but I just couldn't sleep. Other fellows could.

Kinnear: I guess for the first fifteen, twenty years on the job we had running books. It was just a big book, on the edges were your street locations, like Springfield and Hunterdon, and next to it would be first alarm assignment, second alarm assignment, third alarm assignment, fourth alarm assignment, fifth alarm assignment. And then down at the bottom were move-ups. Of course, the first alarm on Springfield would be Six, Twenty, Twelve, and Seven engines and Three and Five trucks. You automatically went when that bell hit. You didn't have radios. Then your second alarm would have the next four engines and one truck that went to the fire. You went automatically. Then when a second came in, you went to your move-up companies. That was automatic, too. The move-up would be Six to Fourteen and you did that automatically.

You didn't have radios. You went to the running book. If it was forty-one twelve, Six Engine's home box, you rolled Six, Twenty, Twelve, and Seven. You went automatically and then you drove all the way to the box. If it was South Orange and Sanford, you went all the way up to South Orange and Sanford. There the Battalion Chief would have to wait until all the companies came in and then he'd wave you up or whatever he wanted. The running books were similar to the cards except the cards had the location on top right, and your columns and you didn't have the automatic move-ups. Move-ups were made by the operator.

Masters: Every man had his turn at the journal. If you had to go to the bathroom, you had to get a guy to take care of the journal. It was where everything was written down. You had to write down the time of the alarm. Then you'd stay awake. When each engine came back you booked everything back, the return call. If we went out to a fire, the captain would write down what we did at the fire. We had no radio. They just had a speaker in the sitting room. That was it. When you came back from a fire, you had to call the operator.

F. Grehl: There was a book. Every alarm was in it and every box had an assignment, first alarm, second alarm and it went right down to fourth alarm. Then the companies were listed on the last two lines in accordance with how close they were to that particular box. Every company that was in the city was listed there as to how they would respond in the event that you had companies that were out. Say, for instance, you had a large fire and so many companies were out that the whole running book first alarm and second alarm assignments were null and void. Then you would go down to that reserve and take them in order. It was all automatic. The house watch was responsible for the response. Of course, the captain is ultimately responsible, but the house watch would say the first five or six or seven companies are out. You would just go down the list. The first alarm is four engines; you'd just take the next four companies.

Move ups were automatic. Across from where the assignments were listed, was another listing that in the event you had a second alarm Six would go to Seven, Six would go to Fifteen, Four Truck would go to Five. They were all automatic and usually there were two engines and a truck that would move up on every second alarm. That book was basically the Bible. It took a long time for them to draw it up. The day after they started taking out companies, Twenty-two Engine, Twenty-three Engine, Thirty Engine, well they were all on that roster, you had to skip a company and so forth. As they started taking out companies you had to learn. A lot of the fellows would go through the book and just cross out Thirty, Twenty-two, and Twenty-three, if they were motivated to do it. There were some places where they just weren't motivated. They could care less. Then they decided to go to the card system because when they made changes they could just put a card in its place. It seemed simpler.

They eliminated the automatic move ups because when they went to the card system the operator made the move ups. The operator would oversee the entire situation and decide where to move up. You could have two fires and you couldn't take a company from Down Neck if they have a second alarm in the Central Ward and the Down Neck company is supposed to move up. That would be automatic if Four was supposed to go to Five Truck, the next one on the second line for the move up, that truck would make the move.

Once you understood it, it was basically simple. But it was subject to mistakes. On the big propane fire that they had Down Neck, Ten Truck went to the fire on the third alarm from Five Truck. Then at around six o'clock they ordered us to go to One Truck's quarters. So, we went to One Truck. When we got to One Truck there were two other truck companies insisting they were supposed to be there under the automatic move up system. Captain Fitzgerald said, "To heck with you. I'll go back to Five Truck." So that's where we went. When we got to Five Truck, there was a whole new crew to come on at six o'clock waiting, didn't know where to go. So Fitzgerald told us, "Go on home, they're taking over." That's where the confusion would lie, when you had a major fire. That's when they decided the operators would take charge of the move ups.

Besides recording the alarms, the man on the house watch had other duties. Taking care of the furnace was a lousy job when we had coal heat. Shake down the ashes; put them in the barrel, and cleaning up. Three or four times a night you had to go down and check the fire, things of that nature. Then you would go out on a run and the fire goes out. Now you have to start another one.

Back then we had pot stoves. Pot stoves are a little stove next to the furnace. In the summer time the furnace would go off. It was steam heat with coal. So you wouldn't run it for hot water in the summer. You got hot water automatically in the winter. Water would be routed through this little pot stove and it would heat the water for your hot water and fill the boiler up. You had to keep the pot stove going all the time. Of course, you were constantly going down there. It was just a little stove. It was the house watch's job to take care of that.

The pot stove always went out on Bernie Havic. You'd wake up in the morning. There's no hot water. It didn't work all night long. Of course, his captain was always on his back. When I first went to Six Engine there was a captain name Captain Goldman and he wanted hot water. They used to say he wanted golden hot water. He had a problem with Havic, like all the captains would, about hot water. One day he says to Bernie, "I want hot water today and I want no excuses. If you have to sit down there all day, you're going to keep hot water going."

Well, about two o'clock in the afternoon we go out on a box over at Fifteenth Avenue somewhere. In all the apartments they had these little gas spiral stoves. They turned the gas on, the hot water was heated, and it went into the boiler tank. All of this was in the kitchen. This little stove was there, the tank, and everything else. That was for hot water. Well, we get there. They had turned it on and then had forgotten about it. The next thing you know, it's building up with steam. We go there. We have an overheated boiler system. You're supposed to light it manually and shut it off manually when you have enough hot water. It wasn't automatic.

Havic and I ran up the stairs with a booster, that's what we had then. We get up there and the captain comes up the stairs and says, "What do you have fellows?" Bernie says, "Come here Cap, I want to show you something." He goes into the bathroom faucet and he turns on the hot water. Nothing but steam comes out. Our job was basically just to relieve the steam pressure. He says, "I got so damn much hot water in Six Engine it's backed all the way up to Fifteenth Avenue."

Vesey: Keeping track of the book was important. When it came your turn, you book all the alarms, the return calls, all of that. Until they final did away with the return calls, which was good. Record all that stuff they wanted recorded. The chief makes his rounds. Chief comes in and you write it down, left this that. Special Service comes, left something, you made note of, kept a record of it. Writing up of what we did at the alarms, the captain or the acting captain did that. The main thing was you answered the phone. You were on the book.

With double companies, we used to do it month by month. That was the best part about a double company. The down watch was a pain in the ass. I was in double companies and single companies. I just prefer the single company. I see some of the guys, they missed the box, missed the second alarm. You're upstairs sleeping. "Don't we get that?" Yeah, that happens.

Masterson: The actual duty was to sit at the desk and stay there. And you write in the journal everything that occurred over the alarm system, what time the alarm sounded; received station so and so. Then the return call, you would write the return calls alongside the alarm, the two chiefs' return calls. On another line used to go all the engines and trucks. You're sitting in Five Truck and monitoring all the Third Battalion. Today, they probably don't do any of that. But then you sat there and you had to write up the whole alarm assignment. Then we had chiefs that would come around and look, check the book. They had their own pad for the times to make sure you did it right, because they knew you were sitting in the kitchen. So, you wrote it down on a piece of paper. Then the clock in the kitchen was different than the one in the watch room. What do you want from me?

We had no radio, but you knew what was going on. The way you knew what was going on was, you'd hear the joker turn over for a second alarm. That's how you knew it. Of course you didn't know what was going on until you got there. Then there's the false alarm. You'd go all the way to the box until you reached it, but on the way in the chief was probably standing in the middle of the street waving so you'd see him a couple of blocks away and turn and go back. But after they got the radio, my God, you went half a block from the firehouse, turned around, and came back. You'd know it was a false alarm. That was a big break. Understand that with the radio, now you can hear the chief reporting in what kind of work they have. You prepared to go because you figured with two two-story buildings going, he's going to bang a second.

Deutch: They had cards that you looked up and a book. So, they were in kind of a transition period then, but we used the display on the wall. I used to make them up with my printer. They were all over, even out on the apparatus floor. Our boxes were out there. We did travel down to Newark Airport and the Elizabeth line. So, we had a big territory to cover.

Freeman: When I first came on the job, we had coal. The guy used to back the coal truck up to a plate in the sidewalk, lift the plate up, and dump the coal into a coal bin downstairs. Don't go down there when he's dumping the coal. The man on watch had to take care of the furnace downstairs. He had to make sure the fire didn't go out. You had the big furnace for the heat and a smaller one for hot water. You had to go down there and make sure it wouldn't go out. You kept it up all the time. I came on the job in 1956 and they had coal. It may not have been too long after that, when they converted it to oil. They didn't replace the furnace. They didn't replace the unit. They just converted it and they put a hot water heater in. They took the old smaller one out.

McGrory: You had your watch and the man on the watch was on the watch. He made sure that everything that went out came back. We had to be very on the ball and everything had to be in that book. When I came on it was a different journal. It was a long journal and every man's name was written in, time in, time out. If you went out to the store, they booked you out to the store. I went out on a signal five one time. I was in Seventeen. It was during the day, in the summer, and some kids came running in saying they saw something. The captain sent me out. "Put your cap on." There were no handi-talkie radios and I had to go down to check it out. I was the Pied Piper. I had about forty kids around me, screaming and yelling, but the captain sent me down. The kids were all over. It was nothing.

Denvir: They had the running book when I came on. Everybody knew if there was a second alarm, you would go. It was automatic move ups for different fires. They were just coming in with radios. Not all companies had them. It was shortly before that, that everybody would roll into the boxes and the chief would just stand there and give a hand up.

Charpentier: We had running books and it was almost all automatic. In other words, if there was a second or third alarm that came in, you looked in the book. What company moved up to where. It was all automatic. And then, I guess, in the '60s they went to the running cards and the discretion of the operators as to move ups or by passing companies if they want. For a while there the Deputy not working the fire, whether it was the First Deputy had the job and the Second Deputy is back, it was at their discretion. They could override an operator, could make what moves they saw fit to keep the city covered.

Miller: There was no radio on the apparatus that I could recall when I first came on the job. That came later. Everything was by return by telegraph, so when you were on the book you were on the book. You didn't dare miss a return call because the next morning the captain would look at the book. Actually the operators were the biggest squealers. If you missed a return call and you called up the operator and said you missed it, the operators would jump on your ass. These guys would be jumping on your ass telling you, "Hey, if you miss another call, I'm calling the captain." If you did, the next morning they would call the captain up and tell him you missed so many return calls. Then you had to answer to the captain for why didn't you book them, especially if it was a truck and you were in a truck company. You couldn't miss it. It was life and death at that time.

Dunn: Okay, when I came on the job they had the running book. We didn't have cards. You used the regular book with all the assignments and we had to listen to the bell, it came over a tape, and the numbers would be punched out on the tape. You would go to the book and get your location. I don't know the exact year, but we switched over to running cards because it was cheaper than the book that they used at the time. It was just the cost of doing it. Several years ago, we stopped using what we called return calls. Because of the antiquity of our system, we don't have return calls. So even though the Newark Fire Department still says they have a bell alarm system in effect with running cards, it's not true because we don't know who is in or out.

We really went to a voice alarm system, probably about 1983. Nobody ever called it a voice alarm. If you don't know who's in or out and the dispatcher says you go, you go because you have no idea who is in or out. We've made a big switch and I don't think anybody ever realized what happened. We still call it a bell system. We have bells in our firehouses and we have running cards and we have an assignment, a rigid assignment, but nobody knows who's in or out. So if you don't listen to the radio, you don't know who goes on the alarm. We really did go to a voice alarm when we stopped using return calls. There are a lot of comments out there about getting new running cards. The City doesn't want to purchase them.

When I came on the job, there were automatic move ups. If a second alarm assignment was called in there was a place in the running book for automatic move ups. I was assigned to Eight Engine and one of the assignments I remember in the book was whenever there was a fire in the Third Battalion, Engine Eight was moved to Engine Nine. There were similar situations like that all the way throughout the city. If there was a fire in the East Ward, a North Ward company was moved in to the East Ward. It worked fine. There was nothing wrong with it.

What has happened now, over the years, is we have done away with so many companies that there are no automatic move ups. We rely now on the operator to give descent coverage to the city, based on his discretion. The whole city at that time was designed on move ups. As companies went out of service you would find that they would try to balance out your city. With the idea that the last fire company in the city of Newark would be the center core city which happened to be Six Engine. If there was one unit left in the city it was supposed to be Six Engine in service.

That's totally changed now because of the way companies have been put out of service, moved, relocated, the scarcity of companies. Right now the operators have their discretion. When they see a void or a hole develop it is their responsibility to try to get some company to fill it. When you don't have enough companies covering a geographic area and you move one company from one area to the other one, you're just creating another big hole. Again it depends on what the operator perceives to be the need. It's worked out fairly well, but there's always a time when move ups aren't being done today like they were years ago. It's probably due to the fact that people just don't pay attention. Our operators, if there's a two alarm fire pay attention. But if we have three companies broken down and one's in the shop or one's closed on rotational closing and one guy calls and says I'm going to the Training Academy, nobody is taking a look at the picture to say what's happening, so voids do develop. As a chief officer, one of the things I try to pay attention to now is when things like that start to develop, we try to correct it. Either by making move ups or to stop something from going on.

Carragher: We were in a house with a Battalion Chief, but everyone had to note in the book if a Battalion Chief picked up something, you didn't put in the book, "Chief Donohue picked up this." You had to write, "Battalion Chief Donohue picked this up." Everything was notated in the book.

They had a book, the running book and everything was in the book. Things were done automatically. I was in Nine Engine when I first came on, if a second alarm came in Down Neck, you would wait for the operator, but you were in the book. Nine Engine would go to Eight Engine on a second alarm. And that's what you did. Maybe Nine would go to Twelve on a second alarm over in the fourth battalion. It was in the book and that's the way they went, by the book. The operators just followed the book for everything. At one time they went automatically, but when I came on they had telephones. You waited for the operator to call you. And also in the book was Thirteen Truck. That never came into service. Twenty-four and Twenty-five Engine were in the book. I don't know for sure, but I believe they were down the port. Twenty-two and Twenty-three were in service until I think 1959 when they put the forty-two hours in. They were in the book.

Harris: When you had the watch everything that came over that bell system you booked. Today the guys don't have to book anything. His captain books, "We went out. We had this fire. We stretched this." But that man, that down watch has no responsibility at all anymore. I think when you took that away, when they said you don't have to do this, you don't have to write up the book, I think they took away another part of the department that they never should have. Because now a guy can come in; go get in the rack; and that's the end of it. He doesn't have to sit up and he doesn't have to do the job where we sat there all night. We didn't sit up. We slept, but when that joker hit, you were looking and you heard it and you hit the bell and you were gone. If somebody came in, you called the operator said, "We're going to so and so, send the box." They don't have to do any of this stuff today. There's no responsibility where that man has to do anything other than what the captain says, "Okay, get the tip let's go, we're going." Drive to the street. Other than that, there's no responsibility for that fireman. I think that stuff should be from the time you come out of the Academy until the time you get promoted. You're in charge of the company. That discipline should be there and we lack discipline on this job today. That's my opinion.

Highsmith: We had cards, we had our first due boxes up on the board, and we had the ticker tape. If we missed the bells, we'd count the clicks on the tape. Plus, we had the house watch book, which in those days, you could go to the house watch book and open up the page to the time and you would read everything that went on. Every engine company that went out, every truck company that went out, you had to put in the book. You had to book them out; you had to book them in. You kept up with what was going on with the city.

McDonnell: There was a book watch and you actually did it. We had a radio in the firehouse, but the alarms weren't announced on the radio. The companies weren't announced on the radio and the companies returning weren't announced on the radio. It was a joker system. It was the same telegraph system we have now. The boxes were sent out the same way and the alarm was mentioned. They gave the alarm and the location of the box. They gave the location. When you did the house watch you had a board and the book. You booked every alarm that went out, every company, signal five, signal eight. You booked the company in, you booked the station, you booked the time, every engine and every truck company and each Battalion and Deputy Chief. You put the alarm, the station, and all the companies.

We would also write like a "T" and then say it was Eight Truck, you would put an eight underneath and you did the same thing with the Engines. As those companies called in service, they would call headquarters. Then it would come over the joker. It would be two clicks for an engine, one, two, for an engine, another two clicks, and then clicks for the engine number and you had to book the time that it came back. The same thing for a truck, it was four and four for a truck and you had to book the time the company came back. That's how you kept track of who was in and out. Because when an alarm came in, you had to know who was out. They don't do it today because it gets announced. But you actually had to keep track of the companies. So when there was an alarm at night, if there was a fire at night, you were up, you had to sit up and listen. Had to make sure all those companies came back. If another box came in, it might be an hour and a half later; you had to know who was out because you might go. So, you actually did a book watch. And you booked the chiefs. I was in a Deputy Chief's house, One Truck had a Deputy.

So you had to keep track of the chief in that house because you had to know if the chief went. He really frowned on you if you had to respond to an alarm that you weren't supposed to go to and it was worse if you didn't respond to an alarm you were supposed to go to. You got hell either way, so you had to pay attention.

Also when the chief came in, the chief came around every day, you booked everything that he took. You booked everything he delivered. You booked that they were in quarters. I think that's one of the things missing in the department. I think that new guys should do the book. Because you learned what was going on in the fire department and it made you take an interest. Guys come in today and they want to watch TV. There are boxes coming in and they're sitting there. They didn't even hear the bells. My whole career I could wake up with the joker. The joker would hit and I would be awake. You had to be that way. There were plenty of nights; we were up all night long on the book. You didn't go to sleep because you had to sit there and you had to wait and listen to those companies. That's something that's changed and I think that's the thing that was lost that they should put back.

T. Grehl: The man on the book was nothing like it is today. He had to answer the phone. I believe on the first ring or before it rang twice, because at that time we didn't have a hot line. The fire department phone was the phone for the operator. It was the phone for everything. There was only one phone line. You had to stay off it; because that was the way the operators conducted their business to you. So, you were only allowed seconds on the phone for personal phone calls. I don't remember a hot line, but I do remember that that phone was important. That's why there was limited personal usage. I don't really remember if you could call anywhere directly from the house phone. I think you might have had to go through the operator. That was obviously before the centrex phone system. But he had to answer the phone.

The box alarms, everything was on running cards. When the box was transmitted, you had to look up the cards. They didn't announce the companies like they do now. So, the man on the book had to know who was in and who was out. It was a couple of years before the companies automatically became available after you declared a three hundred or a three oh five or whatever it was, anything other than a three oh nine. When I came on, if it was a three hundred the operators called six companies, well seven including the Rescue Squad, and asked if they were available. They clicked back on a little joker and that was the return calls. So, when you were on the book, especially at night, you had to make sure if you were covering for Sixteen Engine, they came back in service because the operator didn't say if you responded or not. More times than not there were a couple of extra companies rather than less because you erred on the side of making sure you got there. Otherwise your captain would chew your ass out. But it was important.

I don't know about people walking into the house. The house watch was supposed to be in charge of people walking into the house, make sure they checked in with them. But it was very, very important with the response because you were in charge of who was going to go and who wasn't going to go. Nobody told you until I guess '74, '75. The first step was that you automatically became available. On a three hundred, they didn't have to call you anymore. A three oh eight meant the other three engine companies and a truck company were automatically available. The only thing that they called you on was a three oh nine, which I think is still in existence today. You have to notify them. But I think that was the first step and then about a year later they were announcing who responses, which made the book so much easier.

The chief looked in the book to see if you were recording the alarms. He used to come around. You actually had to log everything in the book. You had certain chiefs who would say, "Okay, last night at three o'clock in the morning they had a fire in the Third Battalion," even though you never covered for the Third Battalion. "What time did Engine Thirteen come back?" They would check. Certain chiefs that were a little pain in the neck would check that to make sure that you were aware because you had to cover for the whole city. But there were more companies, too, a lot more.

Langenbach: Even on Belmont Avenue, the book watch was all your responsibility. In fact, as a new kid, it was maybe almost too much responsibility because we booked every alarm in the city, no matter where it was. We booked all the return calls. You had to keep track of where everybody was. Then when the bells came in, you had to pull the card out.

Look at the card. Everybody had the little board with the companies that were in or out, the in or out board. "Let's see, if Nine Truck's out we get this. If Ten Truck's out we get this." It's a lot of responsibility and it was done. It wasn't like, "I'll sit in the kitchen. If it's a four box, I'll go up front and look." You stayed out there. You pretty much did the book. It was expected that you stayed at the watch desk.

A lot of it went away when we stopped booking all the alarms. We didn't have to do that. Then of course when we went to the radio, radio's going to tell you who are getting this thing. They did announce the companies responding when I came on, but by the time that was being said we were out the door already. Most houses had the board somewhere. Like at Five Truck it was right along the wall by the apparatus with all the boxes that Five Truck got and with first, second, third, or whatever they were due.

I don't know why, but it disappeared. We don't have to do this anymore. Just book the ones you get. So, we lost a little touch of what was going on in the city. And then we became more distant when it was "Let's listen to the radio." You'd hear the bells come in, but nobody even goes to the cards anymore. "Let's see what the radio says and we'll do what they tell us." I think that was a loss for the department.

Luxton: When I came on you had to write down when a box came in. You went over to your journal and you wrote down station whatever it was. Because Six Engine was an engine, you really didn't worry about the trucks, but you wrote down what engines were out. You had a board and slid a little wooden block over that covered over the number so you knew that Engine Seven and Nine and Fifteen and Twelve were out of service. If it was a second alarm, you had the card, you pulled it up and you knew you were going to go. When the people called back in service, there was what they call a joker which is like a clicker on the console. It would click and let you know the company was back. You would have a two, two, and then six. That let you know that Six Engine was back in service. They were available.

You had to listen and record everything in the journal because if you had a chief like Joe Ricca come down, he'd look down at the book. "At such and such a time there was a signal nine for Twenty-nine Engine, Seventeen Engine, and Ten Truck. You don't have it in here, why not?"

I remember we'd be down the basement or playing cards or something like that. The book would be upstairs. Costigan would come up and say, "We have to write the book up. We're missing two hours' worth." He'd call somebody in another firehouse, "Listen, what do you have?" He'd be writing the stuff down, so you'd have the book in chronological order. Or you'd keep it on a yellow pad downstairs so when you got up you could transfer it in there. It wasn't the way you were supposed to do it, but it got done. We had a little ringer on the door, so if anybody came in you knew. You could scoot up from the basement real quick and get to the house watch before the chief got in. Because the engine was in the way and you didn't see somebody coming out of the basement. The way the rig was parked, you could come out of the basement and be at the back of the engine before the chief came in that door to be in the kitchen. So you could be, "Oh gee, Chief, I was just coming out of the door for you. Let me hit the gong for you."

Connell: Book watch, if you're on the book watch you have to sit at the front desk with the book or you could bring it in the back and watch television. You brought the book with you and you had to keep track of every company in the city, every chief in the city. Who's in, who's out.

What time they went out and track all alarms. Everything was booked. We had radios and they announced what units are responding, but you had to pull the card out to make sure what you are hearing is what you have down in the book. There could be a company on a signal five that you might have lost track of or something. So, you could tell by the companies responding if somebody was out that you lost track of or if they came back and you missed the return call. That was one of the first things the chief looked at to make sure everybody was booked in and booked out at the proper times. So, in '74 they're doing it.

Langevin: Back then all the boxes were in little file cabinets. We also had the old bell system. We had the big bell. We had the small bell and we had the joker system. Which meant that the house watch had to keep track of who was out, who was in and when the bell went off, count the bells; pull out the card to see who was going. At the same time, check who was in or out of service to see if we got the run. So, it was the house watch's responsibility to keep track of who was in, who was out, and if we went or not. Return calls and everything else that happened were also booked.

Perdon: You had to do a lot more than you do today. You had to know when everybody came back in. You had to book everybody back in. You had the tape, which came in handy if you fell asleep. You had the tape and a little joker knocking. What you had to do was that you had to book in all the alarms. You had to book everybody when they came back in. You had to know when everybody went out, a signal five not just your company, but a signal five for Engine Fifteen. No matter where it was, you had to book it in. Some of the places had a board, where you could keep track. As they came back in you shut down a light or whatever. We just penciled them back in with the return call. It was a little bit more than you see today, than you have today. It's nice when you just do your company.

Ricca: The night trick, I never slept, for the first year on the job I never slept the nights on the book because you had to make sure you woke the chief. God forbid if he missed a run. I learned a trick with the old ticker tape, how you put a weight on it so when it moved the weight would drop, knock on the floor, and you'd wake up. So, basically for the first year or the times at Nine Truck, I never slept at night.

Gesualdo: The duties of the man on the book were to stay by the book. Don't leave that book. If you had to go to the bathroom, you had to make sure there was somebody there and tell them specifically that you're going to the bathroom. You had to document everything. Everything had to be in the ledger. Even if you didn't respond to an alarm, whatever companies were out, you had to make the entries, Third Battalion, First Battalion, Second Battalion, whatever. You had your running cards. You had to keep track of the running cards to see if you were due on the next alarm due to somebody else being out at another incident. Anything that came into quarters, Special Service, Battalion Chief, visitors, city workers, everything had to be documented. There was definitely more emphasis put on the book watch back then.

We had the tape, the paper tape. Holes were punched in the paper to indicate what box was coming in. You had the bells. You had your joker circuit for when people came back into service. You had to document that. They would send out a signal that that company was back. It was a lot more work. A lot more emphasis put on the book watch back then. Being in a double house, it was a little easier because you had two book assignments and at night you had your down watch guy and your up watch guy. It was a little easier being in a double house. You could just ask somebody to book something for you. "If something comes in, I'm up in the bathroom, book it." But you had to document everything. Everything got documented.

Chapter Three: Camaraderie

Fredette: The camaraderie of the firehouse was great. When a guy wanted to move, somebody would have a truck. All the guys would get together and pitch in to help him move. He wanted to paint his house. They would bring in the drop clothes and paintbrushes. Half a dozen guys would help a guy paint his house. I mean everybody seemed to help one another.

Kinnear: When I first came on the job, you worked I guess it was seventy-two hours a week with the same guys. Then it went to fifty-six hours, which was still a lot of time. So you got to know them. You got to know their problems. You got to know their families. There was a lot more social life then. You'd have dances and you'd have picnics and things like that. You were a tight group.

Everybody or mostly everybody lived in the city then. So you didn't have to travel fifty miles to go to a picnic or go to a dance. Everybody cliqued together. We played softball. It was great. I think the biggest thing was people moving out of town. You couldn't get together as much. The shortening of the hours meant you weren't together as much, so you weren't as close. Today I don't know. I guess if you're a young fireman in a good company like McCormack's son or Johnny Griggs' son, the camaraderie is still there.

Vesey: The tour you worked with was pretty close, especially in a single company. Everybody was different, different characters. Everybody was their own self. We were more or less foot loose and fancy free with the screaming and hollering. We always had a good captain. A couple of arguments here and there, but I'd say ninety-nine percent of the time we got along great.

Masters: The fire department was like a family; at least it was in our house. We always got along and looked out for each other. John McDonald's wife had twins. So John would come in in the morning, he's on the book. I said, "John, what's the matter?" "Ah, one twin was awake. He wakes the other one, so my wife's got one. I've got one. We're walking the floor." I said, "John, go upstairs. I'll take the book." That's the way it was. Want to go home. Go home.

F. Grehl: The camaraderie extended from the firehouse to your personal lives. I think what broke that up was the residency. When they started moving away it was harder to get together for various fire department functions. In the early days, when we used to have dances and picnics they were always packed. We used to have three or four dances and picnics galore. You just couldn't get into places. They were so packed.

That's the comradeship that you had years ago. I don't know if you remember Newt McCauley. He had a fire in his home. He lived in Bradley Court. I worked with him one year over there in Twenty-nine Engine. The whole bunch of us were still good friends because we had some tremendous picnics. They still invited me even after I left for Six Engine. He had a fire on Bradley Court; burned out his entire apartment. The family had six kids. They all got out.

You wouldn't believe the fellows, the firemen who went over there. We went over the next day, cleaned the place out; took what clothes we could to the cleaners and salvaged them; scrubbed the whole place down; dried it out. The next day we went back and painted the whole place. What the firemen did for each other.

Comradeship? You're living day in and day out in the firehouse. You're spending an awful lot of time together. Forty-two hours a week you're spending together. You really depend on these people for your life. You know their family history. You know their problems and everything else that goes on. It's something you really don't know from somebody in an office. You go out and you work together. You know who's doing the work and who's slacking. It doesn't take much to tell them.

We had the Anchor club, which was a Catholic organization. They used to have scholarships for kids and it was open to fire department personnel. You didn't have to be Catholic. Each year a boy and a girl received a scholarship. They got a four-year scholarship. They ran these dances for profits and had fifty-fifties. That's how they got the money to do it.

As people retired and left, the Anchor Club folded. There was a treasurer's fund in the Credit Union that had about six thousand dollars in it. All our scholarships were paid and we have six thousand dollars left over. We divided it evenly between the two chaplains, three thousand to Reverend Bleakney and three thousand to Father Raught to do what they wanted with it.

Masterson: The money wasn't there, but the job was good. That was the only reason you took it because the comradeship, the guys getting along. People loved to come to work. That's what it was in most houses, Twenty Engine, Six Engine. The more work the house did the more the guys liked it and they stayed with you. The busier the house was, the less sick leave there was.

Griffith: Well, I don't know if it was because I was younger and more idealistic or what, but I was fortunate in knowing the firemen and chiefs I did. They were men's men. There was no doubt in my mind that Newark did have the best fire department in the country; couldn't have had better people or better guys. I always felt fortunate and proud in even working with these fellows. The ones that I got to know either playing with the softball team or socially were just great people.

A lot of these fellows who were on the fire department when I first got here were all products of being in the service and that might have had a lot to do with it. In those days this was the job. They were all in town. They got together socially. They got together in all kinds of ways. There was a camaraderie that I could never describe to anybody.

Wall: I think we all experienced the camaraderie of the firehouse. That was a serious part of the job. Guys you worked with were more than just guys you worked with. The forty-two hours took away some of the camaraderie because guys were more detached from each other than they were before. When we all started moving out of town, we took away more. When I first came on the job, we had informal softball leagues. We played the volunteers up in Morris County or wherever. We were really a close-knit group of guys. We all lived pretty close to one another. In Vailsburg there was a cop here and a fireman there. When we all started to move out of town, you were more of a commuter. You kind of lost that.

Freeman: I would say I haven't missed out on the camaraderie of the firehouse. Some might say in the beginning I did, but I don't think so. Because I didn't want to take part in what was going on there. But then the years after that, when we changed captains and the people changed, then I changed. Then we had that camaraderie. We had a good team. It was a team effort and I learned a lot from the guys who were on the job like

Sherman Dubois.   He was a good firefighter.   He was a good engine man, too.

McGee: How much camaraderie you have depends on what firehouse you're in.   I've seen firehouses where they strictly don't talk to each other. Literally don't talk to each other.   And I've seen other firehouses where they're like one big happy family.   I think it always has been this way.   It seems to be automatic that the busier firehouses have the best relationships. Whether that's because you have less time to get on each other's nerves or pride, I don't know.

I think one thing that broke into that closeness a little bit is now guys don't live as close to each other as they used to live.   You were forced to be a family years ago because you saw more of each other.   Now when you have to travel an hour and a half to get to work or something, you're not really going to have the time.   You're coming in as late as you can and not really getting involved in any off duty things because it's too much to travel. It's not that you don't want to have the friendship.   But as far as in the firehouse, I think that most of them are like family.   I enjoyed it very much.

Stoffers: I don't think the camaraderie got deeper.

McGrory: The Fire Department is made up of families within the companies, within the battalions, within the division, within the fire department.   It all depends on where you are and what you're doing.   A lot of the companies are very tight.

What motivates you in an outfit?   What makes the best outfit? Everybody wanting to be in it, it doesn't have to be the easiest place to be or the nicest place or anything like that.   It's the camaraderie, the feeling of getting the job done. The city isn't going to motivate you, so how do you motivate yourself? How do you keep that up? Everything affects the overall outcome of the operations of you as a firefighter or captain or chief, the company, the battalion, the fire department within the city. The camaraderie motivates you.

Denvir: It's like a family. It's just a fantastic way to work. I've always worked with good people; always got along well. Everybody looks out for each other. More so in the busier house, but no matter where you go, you have good firemen. You always run into guys who are good firemen. Fun to be with and they do the job. When they have to do it, they do it. That's the type of job it is.

Freda: The camaraderie was tremendously strong. We had a tremendous social life in that firehouse. We had chess games every night with big arguments. Where people who were passing would think we were completely crazy and we hated each other. You never heard people fight over a chess game like we did. It's supposed to be a calm game. We fought continually. They were cheating. It was fun. It was a celebration of our friendship and we used to do this all night.

When you came to work, you really would look forward to it and you really had a good time at work. I've seen that change during my later years in the field. The biggest change came because of the residency law. That happened when I was a captain in the Rescue Squad. I remember being very concerned about this law they were trying to pass in Trenton that would make it mandatory to live in Newark. I was living out of town at the time and my wife was really upset about it. My wife told me point blank she wasn't moving back no matter what the law said, even if I had to get a legal separation. She wasn't coming back to Newark. This was a real heavy weight on me for a while.

Now when the residency law was defeated in Trenton and it meant you could live anywhere you wanted, a lot of people bailed out of the city. They left and moved all over the state. Then there was a dramatic change as the new fellows come on and the old didn't socialize anymore. You were their friends during their shift and then they went home to their other friends. You didn't have that on- the-job off-the-job friend. It exists to a small extent today. If you happen to live in Long Branch and there's another Newark fireman living in Long Branch you may be a friend of his, you may not.

The Firemen's VFW post on Grafton Avenue was a very active place. It was a building owned by the VFW Firemen's Post. It was a secure area. Every fire department racket was held there. The FMBA and the Fire Officers' Union met there and a lot of firemen and their wives socialized there. That's the difference. Most of the members were Newark firefighters. There was a lady's auxiliary and most of them were wives of Newark firefighters. They went there at night. Instead of going to the local bar, they went there to that bar. They sat there and they drank and their wives came with them. It was a very active post.

You had to be a veteran with those dates that are specified during wartime to be a veteran of foreign war, but most of the guys were. They had parties there. Most of the testimonials for promotion were held at the post. They used to rent it, used to cater it. Everybody went there. It was a safe area. People lived in Newark. Then the area began to deteriorate rapidly around there with the cars getting broken into. The building was burglarized and they moved out.

Now very few firefighters live in Newark and they lost that camaraderie, because the firemen and officers socialized at night. They would meet in one of the pubs in Vailsburg. There used to be a pub right off Belmont Avenue, right in the middle of the ghetto called the Group Pop. It was a famous hangout for the guys from Five Truck and Twelve Engine. We used to go there every night. Eat, drink, and talk and laugh together. You don't have that anymore.

Now there's a distinct difference in friendship. See in those days you would have a friend on the job and off the job. Now I think your preponderance of people have friendships on the job only. When they go home they're all left behind because of the distances they live. They can't socialize together anymore. I think this has had a great impact on the social life in the firehouse. The firehouse has become very quiet, very self-centered, where people seem to be off by themselves more. Back then it was all group activity. Everybody was together, everybody stayed up late. Those things don't exist anymore. I'm not saying they're better or worse, it's just change.

Marcell: We had some good times. Nothing was better than to come into the firehouse and eat with the guys. You have a good time. You work with all good firemen. You know the guys would do anything for you. There aren't many people who have the opportunity that a fireman does because you have the opportunity to save someone's life. You don't do that by yourself. When you rescue somebody, there are ten other guys helping you rescue them. You might get the credit, but it takes a team to do everything. I fooled around an awful lot, but that's how I feel about it.

Dunn: It was different in different sections of the city. You see that same thing still going on today. It's probably very widespread. If you're an outgoing personality yourself and get into a company where it's a family, you start socializing family wise, after hour wise, sports wise, even if you don't like something.   If you live with a guy, you go out and have a couple of beers with him; you socialize family wise; then he says "You want to go play golf one day?" You'll go play golf because he's your friend. But there are a large number of people in the department, particularly for some reason your outer lying areas that never quite get into that type of atmosphere. Why that goes on?   I can't tell you. But I guess if I looked around in companies in the central part of the city, you would also find those few people who separate themselves from the group and just don't participate either.

I think going to fires makes your family a little closer. Because you have something to talk about that's job related. It just so happens to be on the fire department.   When we go to a fire, you come back and you talk about that fire. What you saw, the good-looking woman across the street; you see what this jerky company did; and did you see the dumb thing that guy did. But when you're in a company where you don't go to that many fires, you don't look for these things anymore. It's almost like a mundane type of firefighter. You know, you go in; you do it; you get back in your truck; and you go back to the firehouse. "I'm not going to do that again for two more years." So, there's no real talking about what you just did at that incident.

The residency law hasn't changed the camaraderie of the firehouse for the older group. But to the younger groups coming on, it probably has had a telling effect.   When I came on the fire department in '59 there were probably two hundred people hired. Out of that two hundred people, fifty came from the lower part of Ferry Street, Saint Steven's down. Probably, only ten people came on the fire department from Penn Station down to Saint Steven's church.

I don't know if it's because of the local tavern they hung in or where they got the word from, but there were blocks of people who came on the job very close. So, automatically you're little family group is there, because they came out of a local tavern, like a Joyce's Tavern. Maybe seven people came on the fire department at one time from Joyce's Tavern. Automatically you had a group of men asking, "Where are we going after work? We're going to Joyce's Tavern and have a beer." So, you had your family starting to build.

The people stationed in the Central Ward grew closer on the job, where the people in the East Ward didn't. They stood close because they were in a community. People in Central Ward firehouses stood closer because there was no community outside to go to. They didn't socialize in the community. They got in their car and they would go to Vailsburg or to a Joyce's Tavern. Most of the guys would still go.

Does it still go on today? Probably in the same proportions or a little less than before, people still come out of the firehouse as a group and go to some bar. Some people come out and still go to McGovern's on Friday night. When a new guy goes into that company, he'll go to McGovern's with that group because of peer pressure. What do you say? I don't want to go there? I don't like the place? Or do you say "I want to go to the Hilton in Woodbridge."? I don't find many people who do that when they leave the firehouse. They want to stay within the locality of the city, more so in the East Ward, because we have so many establishments to go to. It's very hard in the Central Ward for four guys, particularly white guys, to say, "I'm going to go have a beer across the street at Bill's." You didn't see that go on too much at Six Engine. They would get in the car and go to Vailsburg. I think that's a very normal thing.

As the change of residency came around I think one of the problems you saw in the socialization on the fire department was the fact that people come from so many different backgrounds. If you don't have the nucleus in that fire company to build that family it doesn't develop. I can tell you companies made up of black firemen who don't socialize at all together because they go four different ways. There just was no nucleus when they first came on, where if two of them were saying "Yeah, I'm going across the street to Bill and Ted's." The other guys probably would have done it. It just didn't develop in that fashion.

Other companies have carried that tradition for a hundred years. But there's always that elderly person in that company who starts off the game plan a little bit. He says "Here's what we're going to do tomorrow night. If you guys don't want to come with me you really don't belong in my firehouse." So, you automatically start to hang out with the guy. I don't mean excessively or anything, but you do form some bonds with that senior fireman

That doesn't happen in some companies today. One of the reasons is that everybody is so diverse. It's very hard to get that little family together. If you don't come on and go into a firehouse like that, the chances are the firehouses that aren't like that will never be like that. It's the luck of the draw when you're coming on the job. Are you a better fireman because you're in Six Engine or Twenty-seven Engine? No. It's just that God put me here and this is where I'm going to stay. It's a nice job. You lose something, but how do you project that image out? To say, "Well, no. You have to come up here." or "You have to make Twenty-seven Engine like what you have up there." They just don't seem to be able to do that.

I have heard of firemen with good leadership skills who have left companies with camaraderie and yet can't make that same family grow again in another company. Even where there's an outgoing personality who says, "This is how I want it. Let's do this and let's cook." It just doesn't seem to work. It seems certain families have been there a long time and they perpetuate themselves. Other ones just can't quite get started for whatever reason.

People retire from slow areas of the city and nobody knows who they were or where they're going and nobody really cares, particularly the guys who worked with them. That doesn't happen where that family contact or image is projected in busy companies. Residency probably was a beneficial thing to have. It created a feeling of comradeship. The fire department was a close-knit military type of unit at that time and it did work.

Miller: I think the most cohesive element of this job is being a comrade. It's almost like being at war. Because when you go to a fire, you are at war. The gun is your hose and the bullet is your water. You become close knit and you won't find that, I don't think, as much even in the police department as you do in the fire department. Maybe you would find it in Desert Storm, that cohesiveness. I'm sure you would. But you'll have it on this job for as long as you're on this job. I mean there's bickering, there's kidding, there's fighting, but the bottom line is most of your buddies will put their life on the line for you or try their best when push comes to shove.

Everybody I ever worked with, when the chips were down, they were there to help. No matter if they were black, purple, green, or blue. That didn't affect them. There was bickering that goes on in the fire department and in the houses, but that all seemed to go out the window. When you had to get the job done, most of the personnel got the job done.

Carragher: The camaraderie in the firehouse was good. It was good. My first week, I think, in Nine Engine, one of the fellows on the crew, Johnny Heinz was moving and they said, "Hey, what are you doing for Saturday when we get off duty? Are you going to do anything? We're going to move Johnny Heinz today." So, we all went and moved Johnny Heinz. I think I got home about four o'clock the next morning. We moved him. We had a good crew and the guys mixed pretty well. I think of the four tours up there, one tour didn't blend in with mine because probably you saw them the least. But they were good. We had a good crew.

Haran: Well, it's just like a family. I mean, you're there forty-two hours a week which breaks down to two fourteen hour nights and two ten hour days in an eight day period. You're there from eight o'clock in the morning to six o'clock at night, from six o'clock at night to eight o'clock in the morning. You're sleeping with these guys side by side in a bunkroom. You're eating with these guys side by side. You're talking about family. You're talking about your kids, the good stuff, the bad stuff. You're talking about your wife, the good stuff and the bad stuff. You get to know the guy you work with as well as your family. This is your second family. You're eating, you're sleeping, you're drinking, you're conversing, and probably any guy on this job, after a period of time, his closest friends become the guys he works with. They start socializing after work. Going to each-others' houses, going to dinners, Christmas parties, weddings, christening, confirmations, bar mitzvahs, whatever it may be. So these guys become your close friends, they become your brothers. It's a brotherhood.

A big part of it is fighting fires together, but I think it's also your relationship with the guy back in the firehouse, the camaraderie, you do this for me, I do that for you. I guess that's what camaraderie is. I don't know; the feeling that you have for your brother fireman.

But at the same time I know that I see guys take some tremendous chances, doing something for somebody they don't know. Putting themselves into a tremendously hazardous situation for somebody they don't know. They think they're in there. We always get that report. They're in there and the guy takes a chance, but you also see it when they know there's somebody in there and they take a bigger chance. And they get themselves in a jackpot. But that's a type of camaraderie too. To me it's a special person. A fireman's a special person, a special breed. I don't think that everybody could do it. There are guys who are doing it, but they're not doing it.

Cahill: Oh, it was fun. It was fun. It really depended on what house you were in. What was the makeup of the people who you worked with. One of the reasons we all stayed together so long in Five Engine was we had so much fun together. We were a very compatible group. After I left Five, went down to the Fifth Battalion and then from there to Twenty-seven, it was a horrible atmosphere. I just couldn't wait to get out of there. Then when I went up to Six Engine with Tartis there was a tremendous turn around. I don't think I had as much fun anyplace, Five Engine, maybe Five Engine and Six, but they're both close.

It was too different kinds of atmospheres, two different kinds of fun. I was the old man up there, where at Five Engine I was just one of the young guys. I had a lot more in common with the people in Five Engine, but I had fun in both places. One of my most enjoyable memories will be the ten years up at Six Engine. It was like a different fire department to me. So, I enjoyed it very much.

We socialized much more when I was at Five because everybody lived in the city. We had basketball leagues. We had a softball league, different firehouses. We had a good basketball league. We played every Saturday up in Westside. It was close. Of course, they also had the bowling league. We had people who were living closer together. It's very difficult to get a guy to travel seventy-five miles even for a retirement party, never mind a basketball game. It was fun. We had a lot of fun.

Highsmith: In my firehouse the camaraderie was great. Like I said, we all knew each other's families. We got together every once in a while. As a matter of fact, the way I got to know a lot of people on the job was because of the fire department ball team. Freddy Scalera and Jimmy Conlon had asked me if I played ball. I told them I played a little bit. I went out for the team and I made the team. I became pretty good playing with them. I played ball all my life. I met guys who I'll never forget. Big Bob Griffith is still on the job. Skippy, Danny from Thirteen Engine, Artie Bragger, Freddy played with me, Jimmy Conlon, John Delk, Stan Pugh. There were so many guys who I met. We used to go every year and play ball in the Eastern Industrial league's tournaments together.

Like I said, the camaraderie was fine. I had no problems no matter where I went to on the fire department. I was the twenty-sixth or the twenty-seventh black to come on the job. But coming on the job I had never let color stop me because I didn't think anybody was any better than me and I didn't think I was any better than anybody else. And I never let the color of anybody's skin separate us because we're all human beings. That's the way it always was. I gave respect and I got respect. I had no problems that way, although I heard a lot of guys had problems throughout, but it used to hurt me. I think when you have problems, you have to be a man to get up on your feet and face those problems head on. I don't go hide. I won't go ask for help. What is your problem? Why do you have a problem with me? Let's sit down and discuss this. Problems like that in Nineteen Engine, never ever came about. We were just friends. That's all we were. We helped each other out any way we could.

Butler: The fire department was a hell of a family years back. Now you still have the family atmosphere, but it's cut down a lot. It's more just within the company or the house rather than citywide. They used to have sports events. One time we had a bowling league in the city strictly consisting of firemen. And you had thirty-two teams of five men, actually you had eight men on a team because you had two men from each shift. So, whenever a shift is working you still had a possibility of six men showing up. You had things like that. Everybody from all over the city knew each other. Always talked or kidded with each other.

Social events were a lot more then. Where you had a lot of guys going to these events, but the biggest thing with that too was the location where the guys lived. At that time guys had to live in the city. Most of them did. Some of them had lived out a little bit, but most of them lived in. They were right there all the time. When the state passed a law that you could live anywhere you wanted, the following year was the last year for the bowling league because of the guys moving wholesale, bailing out of the city.

Cody: Oh, there's definitely a family. You spend as much time here in the firehouse as you do home. You eat with the guys; you sleep with them. It makes retirement very difficult. Just to pull yourself away because you're leaving. You're leaving your family. But a lot depends on who you're surrounded with, the guys who you're working with. You could be with people who you just wouldn't want to be with. I guess that would make it a little bit easier to leave.

They did have baseball teams, which I never got involved in or football teams, but I was on the bowling team. Two Truck had a bowling team. It was from the house, Four Engine, Two Truck. We called it Two Truck and we used to bowl, one night a week. Every house had its team and it was very competitive. It was a lot of fun. It was a night out with the guys.

Garrity: We did everything together. I still hang around with four of them. We still do a lot of things together, Jimmy Cody, Carmine Valano, and Kenny Marcell. We all worked together and we all still see one another on a regular basis. And Dennis Robbins comes in once in a while, so we do see a lot of one another. But it was an extended family. We did things with our families together. If someone had something to do with their house, we'd go do it. Put a roof on, paint the house, whatever had to be done. We were all there and did it together.

Whether it was High Street or Avon Avenue, they still did the same things. I mean when a guy had to move we went and helped them move. The difference was, now guys lived all over the place. When I started on High Street, everybody lived in Newark. So no matter where you had to go it was twenty minutes to get to the guy's house to help him. But now guys are living in Sparta, down the shore, all over the place. I moved to Westfield, so I was living there.

We did socialize, but it wasn't as much. We didn't spend as much time off the job together. We used to have a couple of parties a year. I used to have them at my house. Jimmy Richardson would have them at his house. A couple of other guys had them, different holidays. I always had a barbeque in the summertime. But we still were an extended family. My wife knew the wives of all the guys who I worked with and the kids all knew one another, but it wasn't the same as it was back in the late '60s and early '70s where we actually did a lot of things together. Some of us even went on vacations together.

McGovern: In my experience the fire department is a family. Everybody I've ever worked with, you feel it if somebody dies or gets hurt or has problems. It's different than working in a Post Office or some other place. It's totally different. It's similar to being in the military. You become buddies with guys in the military too, because you live with them. But it's different than working in a civilian type job.

The danger has a lot to do with it. It's a "you watch my back" type of thing. But I don't think it's totally based on that. It's just being together and knowing different personalities and getting along, trying to take care of each other. You see it in slower companies, some slower companies. You see it more so in the busier companies. It's not just the firefighting aspect. It's living together I guess. It's the feeling that you don't want to let your buddy down, that type of thing.

Prachar: I went to Nine Truck where I had Captain Bitter and worked with a fine crew. I never had a problem back then as far as crew because you lived together. You lived together as a crew. You lived together as a family. You had your little spats here and there, but you didn't have one guy who didn't talk to another guy for two months. Everybody just got along together and you did your job. Plus we were busy back in the late '60s, early '70s, so you're always happy. If you wanted to do the job as far as fighting fires, you're always happy.

In a lot of the houses, it was family oriented to the point where you do a lot of things together. Fishing, picnics, when I was in Rescue, we had an annual picnic every year. Go back years ago to Twenty Engine, the real heroes of the hill. Every Christmas, the tour that was working, their families went there for Christmas dinner, to the firehouse. It was cooked. They had a family Christmas party in the firehouse, not with uptown's approval, but it was a family oriented thing. Now if you were to say to the guys, "Let's have a little picnic." Well, what's he buying? What's he buying? The guy's afraid that he's going to spend more money than the next guy.

Go back to family oriented stuff where you love to come to work. You couldn't wait to get in the firehouse. You couldn't wait to be with the guys. Have your wife complaining, "Oh, you'd rather be with the guys at work." "Well, yes. I have to go to work tonight so I might as well leave now." "But it's only three o'clock. You don't have to be in until six o'clock." "Yes, but I like to go in and fool around with this one here or whatever." The atmosphere means a lot. Do you enjoy the people you're working with? Do you get along with the people you're working with? We did things together, family oriented picnics once a year, parties, Christmas parties that included the wives.

You look after each other so the next guy doesn't get screwed. There were five guys in the company. The way we worked our Christmas party was every year we went to a different area. Like I'm in Woodbridge; Jimmy was Booton; Gino was down the shore; Davy Jones was down the shore. Each year we went to a different area so it wasn't a matter of you always had to travel further. That's how it was, but then you go to another house. You don't have that. It hurts. Little things, like to come in every night and cook dinner with all the guys. To turn around and brown bag it, bring in a sandwich at night, that hurt. So, that was like my ups and downs. I'm hoping I'm on my way back up now.

Finucan: What I like most about the fire department will always be when I was fortunate enough to be in a house with the camaraderie of a good house. My own crew at Twelve Engine, we were always friends together. We always had a good house. When I was a Battalion Chief down in the Fifth Battalion, I was just lucky enough to happen to fall into a good house and a good tour. One of the big things in the house was a good cook, very important. We had an excellent cook. This guy was fantastic. He loved to cook. And we had the big dinners every night. Just as it turned out, dumb luck, we get a recruit in. He was a chef before he came on the job. So we had an abundance of all of this cooking. They were always trying to outdo each other with all these sometimes ridiculous gourmet dinners. The camaraderie of being a fireman in a good house would be my most memorable experience.

Cosby: It was like a second family. In the firehouse, you eat together and you sleep in the same room together. You do things more like a family. It's like a family setting and that's what kind of impressed me with it. It was like any other family, you have disagreements, but basically we got along pretty good.

McDonnell: I love the camaraderie of this job. You can't buy this and here they pay you for it. You can't do this. This is better than family almost, almost. Family's a different story. I'm not talking about immediate family. I'm talking about cousins and stuff like that. These guys are like my brothers almost. I feel that close to them. It's like the army. You take the hill because the guy behind you depends on you and the guy next to you. That's who you're doing it for. That's the way I feel when I go to a fire. God knows that's what keeps you going. Plus there's that feeling of self-satisfaction, let's face it. You go to a fire, knock that fire out, you come back, you feel good, you accomplished something. There aren't too many jobs like that where you can get that satisfaction.

But you did it for the guys who you worked with. You worked in the busy companies where you didn't want to let the other guy down. You felt like "I have to do it. It's my responsibility to do it." It's something that should be done. It's very dangerous, yes, but it's something that's necessary and should be done. The morale on this department when I came in was phenomenal. They had more spirit than the Marine Corps. And it's absolutely necessary for people to have that to perform well on this job. Without it you really can't do the job well. Because there's no way that you can pay anyone enough to do it, money has nothing on this. It has to be that inside the person to do it.

That spirit was great when I came on. It was wide spread when I came on the job and it still exists, I think, today. The morale has died tremendously. From what I hear it's worse than even three years ago when I left the job. I saw that. I saw that a lot. That it wasn't the way it was. That it had eroded over the years. But there are still pockets of it. There are still some guys who have it, some houses, where I worked they always had it. When I left I kind of thought that some of the tours didn't have it. My tour, I think had it. They were young guys and they felt they still had that spirit. They still had it. There are still pockets of it. There were places where it never existed. It never existed Down Neck, I don't think. Basically, it was the Central Ward, the center part of the city and evidently it was there before it was really busy.

The competition went way back. You hear the stories and that went way back. It wasn't something that just came in the '60s or in the riots. It was way before then that it existed. I think today it's a lot less widespread, a lot less.

The different companies would socialize in the center of the city. We did a lot more socializing. Guys going for lunch to this firehouse. Who'd come down. You had sometimes three or four companies for lunch. We used to go to Nine Truck all the time, Six Engine a lot, once in a while with Ten. You knew a lot of guys. Guys used to come in and out of the firehouse a lot, guys from other tours. That was another thing. Guys would get off their tour. They would sit around and talk firefighting. Guys from other houses would come, stop in. Guys would visit all the time. You would always have visitors at night, people coming in at all hours of the night. They would be out at the bar and the bar would close. They would then come to the firehouse.

It was a lot of camaraderie during that era. Guys were very close. Danger. There was a lot of risk, a lot of fires and I felt even as a captain when we used to get on each other's nerves. I'd say "We need a fire." It was a tension breaker. It made you get a little closer. You just went somewhere you had to count on this guy to save your life if something went wrong. There was a lot of esprit d'corps on the department.

Pianka: The camaraderie on this job is hard to duplicate anywhere. You're not going to have that anywhere. Some of the best meals I've ever had were in the firehouse because it's such a casual thing. Guys go out of their way to cook. They try to find out things, cook something special. It's like a big boys club only better. You feel like you're with brothers and cousins. It's a big family. We all realize what we are, who we are. A lot of times you suspend the rest of your life for those twelve hours or ten hours that you're here. It's like you're in a never-never land. You know you're here for these hours. So whatever happens, wherever you're going to go, there's no big rush. Life is easy.

It's like we're going downtown today. Well, we have to go do this and that, so what? I have all day to do it. That contributes to it. It's not surreal, but it is separate from the rest of the world. Hey, some guys, you live with them long enough. Your family grows. Your families get to know each other. They grow up together. It's great being with the younger guys. I would never want to be with a bunch of old guys. It's best to have a mixed company because we offer each other something. Guys look to me for advice for different things and I look to them for other things. So, it works. It's a generational thing. Even if it's just finding out who the rock star is on TV. Well, they're there to know it. They know it. It's not like it's a bunch of old guys, "Ah, turn it off." We'll sit there and watch it. I'll learn something from them. I mean maybe it's trivial, but that's the way it is.

The parties are great. Let's face it. You go to a cocktail party and half the time you don't know three quarters of the people. I'm talking to my sister one day and we're talking about a funeral. And I told her all the people who I know. She says, "Gee, you know a lot of guys." I said, "I've got news for you. Out of five hundred guys on the job, I could easily converse with two hundred and fifty to three hundred of them, no problem, because we know each other." I said, "The other two hundred, we could sit down and we'll find things in common." She said, "You know, that's so impressive. That doesn't happen in the real world."

Rotonda: It was fun. The biggest thing, I think, is working with good firemen. Like to me I worked with Al Payne, Mike Joyce. They were good fireman. Most of the guys were all conscientious too. You learned a lot from them. Everybody watched out for everybody. That's the way it works. That's the way it has to be. We still get together once in a while. The guys go out to dinner and stuff like that.

The only thing I did have to do was I found that I was the only Italian down there with all those white guys. I had to teach them how to eat. When we had to work Christmas and stuff, my mother used to make homemade ravioli for everybody and we took over the whole deal of cooking with the help of my mother, the ravioli, the ante-pasta, everything. Because you guys aren't noted for your culinary arts as much as us Eye-talians are. I used to kill them. Everybody used to eat until they couldn't move. We'd have Ten Truck, Twenty-nine Engine, the chief was Bohringer and his driver. The guy from the drug store across the street used to come over to eat with us. He'd come over every year. That was where I think Jerry Lewis worked, in the drug store years ago.

Then if you were lucky enough to have a guy who knew a little bit about electricity, they start putting in trip switches or direct lines. You had firemen doing more work in the firehouses then. Today, I don't think you can get the same thing out of firemen; to do work in the firehouses like we did because we did it for ourselves. It made it comfortable, so we can enjoy being there. Why make it an ordeal when you can make it more of a pleasure? That's the way it was. You had the guys pull together and do a lot of different things, help each other out. Some guys, if they procrastinated, the other guys got on them, so they would move either way. But you got things done.

T. Grehl: Camaraderie on this job? Oh, without a doubt, without a doubt. And the busier companies were, the closer you were. My contention always was if you were in a slow company and didn't put that spoon away, I was going to sit there and say, "Why don't you clean up the table and put your spoon away?" Well, that would be stewing there because it might be there for two hours while we're just looking at each other because we're not in a busy company.

In the busier companies that spoon might only be there an hour because now you're going to go to a fire or you're going to go out even if it's a false alarm. In the busiest company that spoon's going to be there fifteen minutes and you just finished breaking your ass with somebody at a fire. So now the spoon issue isn't even important because you just made a second floor or stretched fifteen lengths of four inch and inch and three quarter, now you took it up together. Who cares about the spoon? Throw it in the garbage when you get back. It's not an issue anymore. Where in the slower company they would brood and brood and brood.

When I first came on I was Down Neck. They were a little older. So, I would leave the firehouse and go play in a softball league. Where they would go home and be with their wives and the family. I had a wife, but I had no family at the time. So, your interests were different. But when I got to One Engine, then I was with younger people, had more in common. You would go out with the wives and have dinner. Then when I made the next step to Six Engine, again we were all closer. Now those people, our kids grew up together and I went to the weddings of the children not only to the confirmation, but now just recently to the wedding of one of them. So, that friendship and camaraderie still exists.

But the closeness, when you go to a fire you can't replace that. When you're just sitting there, it's "Well, I swept the floor yesterday. It's your turn to sweep it today." Plus, in the slow company, we didn't eat together, very seldom. When I went to One Engine we all ate. When I went to Six

Engine we all ate. When I went back to Twenty-seven, years later, I instituted trying to eat together because they still didn't do that. Try to build relationships, but when you're slower it's not the same.

J. Ryan: Life in the firehouse, the camaraderie always was terrific, both on and off the job. There was never any question about who wasn't invited or who was invited or who was going to be there. Everybody was there. There were very few problems in the firehouses at the time.

Connell: You work with guys and learn to admire them. I worked with Sam Pappalardo. I still have a lot of admiration for the man. He is a great truck man. He's a good guy. No matter what he does, he can get away with it. The thing that made me and Sam really close was while we were in Seven Truck together, we were responding to a little piss pot job. We were driving down Park Avenue. As we approached Clifton Avenue, he saw his son standing there with a couple of his friends. We went to this little one room job. We had it out in less than half an hour. On our way back he asked, "My son is there. Can we stop and talk?" I said, "Yeah, no problem." As we're coming back to the firehouse after the fire, we stopped and he was talking to his son for about half an hour or so. We finally made it back to quarters.

I had a something to do the following morning, so I left around seven-thirty when my relief came in. When I came back in that night they told me Sam got a call about eight-thirty in the morning telling him they found his son dead in bed. He had walking pneumonia. Sam went through quite a rough time after that. I think the fact that I just let him stop and talk to his son on the way home that night grew a special bond between us.

Langevin: I think the morale was pretty high. Everybody did their job and did it well. Firehouse life was pretty good. Almost everybody got along. Back then I think that more guys stuck together a little bit more off the job. A lot of guys might possibly work part-time together and attended more family functions together like christenings and weddings, things like that. You don't see that too much nowadays. I don't know why.

When I was in Vietnam, I was on a river patrol boat, crew of four. The same thing, we ate, slept, worked, and fought together. I was in combat for a year. I liken actual combat to firefighting, fire being the enemy. You either kill the enemy or he's going to kill you. So the guys on my crew on the fire department were like my boat crew. We're going after the enemy. Over the years a lot of guys came in and went. Some guys stuck around. The guys who stick around, I think, the longest, get the tightest. I made a lot of friends on Avon Avenue, a lot of friends.

Perdon: The time I spent at Six Engine was the best time I've ever seen in the fire department. I mean even the interaction between companies was so much better than it is today. You just didn't have time to be candy ass about anything. The pet peeves and all the arguments that you see even in houses now, you didn't have time to do that back then.

As busy as you were, you still got bored at times. The year we did those five thousand runs, on average it worked out to a working fire a day, but you know in the real world it was maybe three here in one day. Then you went about a month before you caught another one and you were climbing the wall. Even as busy as it was, thank God we were young. You were still looking for more.

You didn't realize it at the time, but the morale was great. You compare it to nowadays and what's going on, it's a whole different ballgame, completely different ballgame. It was nice. It was fun. I hated vacation. I really did. I hated going on vacation. I never called in sick. Never took a personal day. They forced me to start taking personal days, I just had so many. I'd work for anybody. Never worried about getting paid back or want to get paid back. It was fun. To me it was fun.

The camaraderie was good. It was good. Sure you have a rare argument or something like that where they really got mad at each other, but it was like a fleeting thing. It happened and it was done. Nobody really carried or held a grudge for a long time.

Bisogna: I walked in the door at Twenty Engine and it was the United States Fire Department. It wasn't the city of Newark. (laughter) They said, "Welcome to the United States Fire Department. You're in the best firehouse in the city." I figured, "Yeah. Okay. What else are you going to tell me? You're in a dump." It was. There was a lot of camaraderie there. It was about five to ten years ago, they had a Twenty Engine reunion. I'm probably one of the youngest guys left.

It was the only place I've ever known where you could go on detail or overtime on all four tours and you didn't pay to eat. They treated you like you were a brother and they made you feel right at home. Everybody walking in the door, really, they were known for that. Being real outgoing. There were parties. It was a pretty wild place for a while, as a lot of firehouses were back then, but they always got the job done.

It's not so much where you're working or with what equipment, it's the guys you work with. And then how busy you are also. In a busy firehouse there wasn't any time for bickering. Guys got along much better when they're going out the door to fires all the time because you're working hard. You're feeling good about yourself. You felt good about your crew and when you came back, you discussed what happened and where you were at the time. What this crazy lady said or what that crazy captain said. It was a lot more camaraderie than you found in slower companies.

Guys start to worry about whose coffee cup is theirs and who left the paper on the floor and that's my newspaper and that kind of stuff. I saw that when I went from a busy place to a quiet place. Never mind that, in Twenty Engine, the captain's motto was "Attack, attack, attack." In another engine company, the captain's motto was, "Oh, we'll take a two and a half to the back." He's thinking of protecting property in the rear, where the other captain is saying, "Let's go have a good time, break some stuff up, and put the fire out at the same time." It was a different mindset, let's go in there, knock it out, and get it over with. The other guy is willing to sit there and squirt water in the window.

As a fireman you have to do what the captain says. You get both sides of the street. I was lucky enough to be able see both attitudes. I think being in a busier place is more fun, because you definitely get along better with everybody. Before I got promoted I went to Vailsburg for a while and there were three companies up there. I was in Twenty-one temporarily, then I got assigned to Twenty-six after being up there about a year. I switched with Teddy Holod who wanted to study with Ronnie Ricca and I was having a little trouble with the captain at Five Truck for a while, so I switched with Teddy. Then I put in papers to stay up there. I'd say half the guys up there were older than I was. There were a few younger guys. Some contemporaries, Ray Frost, Jackie Hanrahan, we got along good.

It was slower and that's when it set in "Who's cooking?" and he's grumpy because you picked a piece of food out of the dinner before it was ready, and the guys' are yelling, "Well, you didn't get lunch." If you went to more fires, that wouldn't have been there. It would have been easier to get along.

It got cliquey. The guys in the truck didn't talk to the guys in the engine. The old men who didn't want to know; who went up into their room and didn't come out. I remember one night, Eddie McCarthy, a hell of a guy, Jackie Denver, they were the captains. They decided to end some of this animosity that was going on between some of the guys because it was escalating. Not to fist fights or anything like that. He wouldn't say hello to you when you walked in in the morning. That's great. You tell me you're not going to talk to me, the first thing I do when I walk in is, "Hey, how the hell are you?" And the guy would start to steam. I'm going to rub it in now. "What's the matter? You don't want to talk to me?" And sit right next to him. I'll bust your balls. What the hell.

So, Eddie decided to get us all together. He banged the bell one night, eight o'clock after dinner. Everybody came down to the table. He said, "All right guys sit down." Just about the whole three companies were there. That's I think why he did it. And he said, "All right guys let's throw everything out on the table and we'll talk about it like grown men. And we'll see if we can put all of this behind us." Not that it was horrible. Some of it was an uncomfortable situation.

Well, I'll tell you, so much came out on the table. Eddie was shaking his head. He said, "Wow, this ain't going to be over." Because now guys are like red in the throat, blood vessels are bursting and they're screaming at each other. He and Jackie Denvir just looked at themselves. Well, hey we gave it a shot. Like I said these guys were old timers. They were ready to retire. They had thirty years on the job and they were more concerned about who's using their coffee cup and you're reading my newspaper. I mean there were arguments over who took the coupons out of the Sunday paper. I mean the Sunday paper cost fifty cents and I don't know how many coupons you got in the paper. But that was cash to some of these guys.

Ricca: We used to have a picnic with Five Truck, the Tact Squad which rode out of Twenty Engine at the time, and Six Engine on the third tour. We had our own little picnic. Guys socialized a little more. People lived in the area. I watched as it slowly changed. Kenny Miller moved down the shore. Ray Frost eventually moved down to Islin. Pete Romano moved out to Roselle Park. Ray Stoffers moved down to Helmetta which nobody ever even heard of when he came in and told us that story. And I moved to Bloomfield, so we spread apart. But every awards dinner, every Credit Union dinner, we always got together and had a good time. The bad times, Ray Frost got buried twice. That's probably the worse thing I remember.

Sal DeFranco kind of summed it up on his last day when he retired. "I ain't going to miss the job. I'm going to miss the guys." Well, now it's kind of the other way around because the guys, unless you're in a good company, guys don't gel like they used to. You live in the firehouse. You eat in the firehouse. You become brothers, you really do. No matter what anybody says, there's a closeness that just isn't there anymore. Not in my particular house or Five Truck, but I sense it at other places.

I think the busier the company, the more you gel. We used to get on everybody else's case. When you don't have a fire in a while everybody's nit picking. Like, "Where's my coffee cup?" "I was reading the newspaper and you came along and took it." You bicker, but it's a good bickering. It's a bickering because more or less you're saying, "Give me a fire. I want to work." What I usually do when I see that happen, is go and drill. It gets a little bit out of everybody's system. But believe me, the busier you are, the more fun you have. You just feel good. You feel good about yourself. You feel good about the company.

Camaraderie, never being a Marine, but working around some of the nuts that were, like Frankie Bellina to name one. Ray Rivera is a jar head. I guess that's the slang that they don't like to be used, but I would have to compare it to a Marine in battle. We lost the after work get-togethers because guys just don't live around each other anymore so you can't take off to maybe have a beer at the local bar or tavern after your shift. But I've seen guys hurt and other guys put their hands in their pockets immediately to buy tickets. Jimmy Weiss is putting an addition onto his house. Guys show up, work for him all day for a beer and a sandwich. I guess because, not to be corny, but I guess because we face death in every fire we go to, it makes us closer.

It's like no other profession in the world, other than maybe being in the service where your life depends on the guy next to you. It's absolutely true and it goes as far as backing apparatus in. You're looking out for the other guy. "Hey, somebody's coming around the truck. Watch out." It goes from writing the book up, to rolling out the door, to having them sitting down having lunch together. A guy gets up to get a paper towel for himself. He gets five, one for everybody. And guys do it subconsciously. Somebody gets up to get a soda. "Who wants a soda?" It's what I have over at Twelve Engine. I'm assuming most of the other units feel the same way about each other. It's the shoulder to shoulder work that makes you love the guy next to you. And it is; it's love. It's not just a friendship; it's love.

The fire department is more than family; it's immediate family. You know Jack's son is having his tooth pulled. Joe's son has been running a fever. The damn stories of my kid hit a home run, my son, my son, my son. Once again, I guess because I miss him so much, Ray Frost would talk about his wife and kids from the minute he came in until the minute he went out and rightfully so. He ended up with kids to be proud of and a family to be proud of. But you knew everything about everybody. You showered together. You went to the bathroom together. You're actually closer to some of the guys than your wife. Everybody knew everything. Once again, I feel I still have that in my company. I don't know if other companies get along as well, but the element that's missing is after work get-togethers. I definitely used to like the after work stuff and the wives knew each other. The kids played together. You lost that and my reason for that I think is because people just all moved away. That would be the only thing that's missing.

I watched guys change. I came on the job; I didn't have any kids. Kenny Miller and Pete Romano, Ray Frost, your brother had no kids at the beginning. I watched young guys go to old men with gray hair and beards and crazy ideas about living in the mountains or skiing the slopes or watching Pete Romano afro pick his hair in the mirror over the sink at Five Truck because he was losing it. It's stuff that your wife notices about you. You notice that about the guys you work with. You say, "Holy shit! Kenny Miller looked like he's a million years old the last time I saw him." Kenny Miller's home telling his wife, "Well I saw Ronnie Ricca. He looked like he was eighty."

You knew everything about everybody and everybody is there for you. One time I broke my hand playing softball and I'm a smart guy, so I went to set it myself. I transverse the bone and had spun it around. So, I had to have an operation. I was in Columbus Hospital. I woke up out of recovery. The whole crew was around me making sure I was all right and Jeannie was all right. The guys you work with were the guys who mean the most.

Gesualdo: Oh, everybody envies us. They still envy us to this day even with some of the problems that we have, with different cultures, different races. But a very close friend of mine always reminds me, he was a police officer in New York and he always envied the fire department because of the camaraderie, the family thing. Just knowing that everybody was welcome, not just firefighters, but he would come in from walking his beat. He was in Brooklyn I believe at the time and he would always be welcomed into the firehouse, coffee, donuts, whatever, meals. And he always said that, he picked the wrong career. He should have been a firefighter.

Where all you have to do is say something like, "Oh, man I have to dig this hole tomorrow to put in a foundation." You have four or five guys there helping you. He said it wasn't that way on the police department. I remember when I worked with the linemen with Public Service, it wasn't that way. You might get one guy say, "Oh, I have the weekend off. I'll come down to help you." In the fire service, it's probably one of the best perks in the department. Thank God it's still there, maybe not to the degree it was, but it's still there. And it's something that will hopefully last forever now.

Chapter Four: Studying

Redden: I was in Two Engine and I guess around 1950, the Second Deputy Chief rode out of Two Engine also. There was a Deputy Chief by the name of John Wilkinson. His driver retired and he asked me if I'd be his driver. So, I drove him as a Deputy Chief. I got a lot of good experience at fires. He was a real great guy. In fact, he's probably as much responsible for me becoming Chief as anybody. He was a friend and an officer. I'd watch him size up a fire and direct a fire, then I would ask him questions about why did we do this, why did we do that. He was great.

Driving the deputy broadened my horizon. It broadened my experience to see companies operating at a big fire. Also it gave me the opportunity of noting good officers and bad officers at an operation. Which is very, very important later on when I was in charge of the fire. I knew the officers. I knew the Battalion Chiefs. I knew the Deputy Chiefs. I knew who I could depend on and who I couldn't depend on, which is a big thing for someone handling a fire. And of course at that time too, I went to Delahansy Institute, it was in New York. Officers from the New York Fire Department ran the school, a promotional school. I went there studying for promotion for captain and it helped out quite a bit.

The captain's exam I took was a true and false, maybe some multiple choice, a hundred to a hundred and twenty-five questions, and there was also a physical involved. I did very, very well in the written. In fact, I got the highest written. I didn't do that great on the physical. I came out ninth on the list for captain. I was appointed with the first group of ten or eleven.

When I was studying for Battalion Chief, I was also conducting classes for guys who wanted to become captains. Of course, that's going to help me because I'm studying to be Battalion Chief. When we worked the two days, in the afternoon we would have sessions where I would do the results of the inspections I made and then we would discuss other things about taking exams. I used to go through books and make up questions and so forth.

The Battalion Chief's exam had a written, time in rank, then an oral examination. There was an oral exam for Battalion, Deputy, and Chief. I had three years seniority. I was a captain from '54 to '57. With the Battalion Chief's exam, of course, I gave away a lot of seniority. Again I had the top written. I didn't do that great in the oral part of it. I came out seventh. I wasn't appointed with the first group. I think in the first group there might have been four Battalion Chiefs made.

The Deputy Chief's test had a written, that was multiple choice. I'm quite sure it ran either a hundred and twenty-five or a hundred and fifty questions; record of service so I had two years as Battalion Chief; and an oral. I came out fourth on the list. I had the highest written again. I didn't do that great on the oral. I'm having a problem with orals. But the first four on the list were made so I was made right away. I was assigned to the Second Deputy.

The test for Chief of Department was essentially the same as the other promotional tests I took. To prepare for it I went to Queens College in New York. They had fire administration courses. And I worked with a Chief from New York, Chief Charles Walsh. He was a Deputy Chief in New York and he taught at Queens College. Then we went to the personnel department in Newark and developed a course and Rutgers picked it up. So, I was teaching at Rutgers when I was a Battalion Chief. I taught Fire Administration for Rutgers in the Newark Campus, down Cherry Hill, and down in Camden. At the same time I'm running a promotion course for a group of my friends, like Freddy Grehl, Vince Greely, and Larry Caufield. Doing all of this teaching helped we assimilate information. Then I took the exam and I had the highest written again and the highest oral.

I trained and worked like anything on the oral. Vince Greely and Freddy Grehl used to come to my house and they'd give me an oral. This went on for a long, long time. Then they would critique it. Not only what my answers were, but how I answered, what my demeanor was and so forth. Those two guys deserve a lot of credit for me becoming Chief because they taught me how to do an oral. Essentially, I thought going into an oral all you had to do was answer the questions. But your tone inflection, things like that mean a hell of a lot.

Kinnear: The first test I took for captain, on which I finished forty-seventh; seniority was two; physical was three; and written was five. So they gave the same percentage rate, fifty percent to seniority and physical that they did to the written. I think seniority stayed at two all along. I don't think that's changed. I would have made it on that first one except for the physical. I didn't realize you had to put that much into push-ups, sit-ups, the Russian dance, and things like that. So I got an eighty-five and a few of the fellows who I beat on the written, who I beat by a couple of points, got in the ninety's, ninety-fives, ninety-sixes. So with the weight for the physical being as high as it was they beat me out on the exam and were made. Where I finished forty-seventh and wasn't made. They made thirty on that list. That was it for the first exam. Then they started gradually changing it to where they downgraded the physical and now they've eliminated the physical all together. When I say physical, it's not the medical part of it; it's the push-ups and sit-ups. I guess now it's two for seniority and eight for oral and written.

F. Grehl: The first promotional exam I didn't take serious. I didn't study. In fact the biggest mistake I made was I let myself get out of shape. When it came time for the physical, I got about a seventy-eight physical. I couldn't do anything. I had an eighty-five written, so I still came out thirty-four or thirty-three on the list. I said, "All I had to do was the physical and I would have made it then." Then all of the sudden I said, "This is worth studying for." So, I started studying. Of course I was married then, too. I was only on the job two months when I got married. So, I guess that's where the big change came in; when I settled down. Said, "Hey if I'm going to stay here and I like it here, I might as well make something out of it." But the difference in rank then was only six hundred dollars.

When I was studying, I was going to Queens College in New York. The teacher was Deputy Chief Walsh. He'd written a book which they used extensively in a lot of the questions for examinations. Vince Greeley, Larry Caufield, Jimmy McCormack, and I were going to school at the time over there. An hour lecture and then we'd have a break, another hour of lecture, a break. We had a three hour session each day that we went.

Masterson: Promotions? It took me twenty years to figure, forget the books; study the questions. You couldn't study the books on the fire department. If you get a set of fire department books, the NFPA and all those other chemical books and these books and hydraulics books, you get all that education, I tell myself, "What the hell am I doing on this job? I can go out and be a professor somewhere if I knew all this stuff." Because you never used it. I found out that you study the questions and look up the answers. Research the answers; keep constantly researching because they had a funny way of asking the same stuff all the time. So that's what struck me, otherwise I'd still me riding the back step. Study the questions, other than that I took a couple of courses in hydraulics.

But promotions, they say it isn't hell if you know the devil. That's an old saying which is true. There was one time there, they made Battalion Chiefs and Tommy Melody was a captain at Eleven Engine. They came to the end of the list. There were maybe ten more to go before they even got to Tommy. So, he figures, well, he's tired. He's been on the job a long time. He goes up to Vailsburg. He transfers. He's not going to study anymore. He's going to put his last couple of years on the job in a slower house.

Somebody made a move downtown. They made ten more. Tommy Melody is a Battalion Chief. Another guy they'd go up there, they've got room and they stop short if they don't want to make somebody. I saw a Deputy Chief's list come out one time and the guy who topped the list was Albright. Whoever didn't like him, somewhere along the line, didn't like him so much that they let that list go for the two years and die. Nobody was made. That's how bitter it could be at that time.

Wall: When I first started studying, studying was like it should be. At that time there was no published list of books, but everyone knew that whatever was the current thing they'd be hitting. You know, the Oklahoma series, Fire Chief's Handbook. At that time a Chief from New York was very popular on the circuit, Charlie Walsh. In fact, a lot of our questions that were on our Battalion Chief's test came from Charlie Walsh's material.

I always studied independently. I never belonged to a group. But I thought I was playing politics when Caufield's brother asked me to join his little group. I figured I'm going to cover all my bases with that study group. We used to meet in Freddy Grehl's house. You'd be responsible for dissecting a certain portion of Fitzcrosby or the Fire Chief's Handbook or Oklahoma and then making questions up from it.

I remember my poor wife used to type the questions. At one time in the firehouse someone stole my book of questions and answers. So, Dorothy and I sat down and we typed up bogus questions and answers. It looked good unless you were a student. It really looked great. And the funny thing is, years later some guy's telling about a drove of good questions and answers he had gotten on a civil service test. And a lot of them were the phony questions I had made up. Because I took them home to her and she recognized them. She says, "I know where this is from. I typed them." That was the question and answer boys. Still are, I guess, they think they have the keys to the kingdom.

I could never learn by rote. If you give me something to study and I understand it, then I don't care what kind of question you ask me on it. I'll answer it. But I was never the kind of guy who would be able to sit down and say, "This is the answer to that question." I can't learn that way. It always held me in good stead because I came out first on my captain's test, first on my Battalion Chief's test, first on my Deputy test. And usually no one came near me on the written. You know how close points usually are. I would say that normally I topped the next guy by eight to ten points. The guy who came the closest was Angelo Ricca. He came within five points of me on our Deputy's exam because I was worried about the union instead of worrying about myself.

That process didn't help me at all when it came to the exam for Chief. I think there were eight guys eligible for the Chief's exam. When we took it, the highest seniority guys flunked which was really unusual. Usually they don't flunk anybody on an exam for Chief of Department. It was the first time that they didn't have a written. There was no written. There was no credit for schooling. There was just an oral. And the oral exam was not based on the orals that I had been familiar with where they asked you a question and the whole premise was that you could give them an answer that showed you knew the material and that you could defend your position. So they could see you were a thinking person. There was no right or wrong answer on how you fight the fire, but you had to show a logical sequence in going through the steps of size up, whatever. And they asked you nasty questions, could you defend those with logic behind it?

Well, our oral exam was questions that later I found were just taken from a textbook. Because when I went down to challenge it I was given the text book and shown where this answer was. For example, they had, "What does leadership mean to an officer?" And I gave them Leadership one oh one, right down the line. They took it from the textbook where there were like seven items and you had to answer each of those seven items. You got so many points if you answered all seven. On my other orals I had always gotten a ninety. I ended up with I think a seventy on the oral. I came in third. O'Beirne was first; Kossup was second; I was third.

That's when I decided it was time to look for a job and I left the Newark Fire Department. Because I realized they probably cut a deal with Stanley because he was number two on the list. For the first time in the history of the Newark Fire Department two chief officers were ever made off the same list. They made O'Beirne. O'Beirne lasted about eighteen months, whatever it was and just before the list died they made Stanley. So, about that time I started looking for a job. And as the old Irish saying goes, "God closes one door. He opens another."

I never regret having left Newark because economically, socially, mentally especially, I was a hundred percent better off going with the Feds. Things worked out beautifully for me. But I was disappointed because everybody wants to be Chief of their own department.

The most radical change in testing was when Carl Stoffers and I come out first and second on the captain's exam. That's when they started doing the multiple multiples. They would ask you a question and there would be several segments to that question. Answer "A" would be "A and D" are correct, "B and C" are not, "B and C" are correct "D" is not. So you couldn't guess the material. You had to have a fairly good handle on it. It wasn't saying, "That's the obvious one. That's obviously wrong, so it's between these three." Prior to our exam, captain's exams used to have a hundred and fifty guys on the list. We had twenty-five. Only twenty-five guys passed even marking on the curve. That's when they started using those questions.

My Battalion Chief's exam was a little different. Because at the time they had brought out a new radio procedure manual in Newark and I forget, something else having to do with rules and regulations. So even though we sat with other towns, let's say they ask a hundred and twenty-five questions of all candidates, the Newark guys had to stay for an additional twenty-five on our rule book and our radio procedures.

I made captain in '62 and went to purgatory. After I came out of Rescue Squad, they sent me to Sixteen Engine. I recall to this day, Joe Redden says to me, "We're sending you to Sixteen Engine. Anybody can be a captain up on the hill, but I'm sending you down where I need you." I said to myself, "Boy, are you bullshitting me, Joseph." Sixteen Engine was his old company. Slow house, they didn't get along with the truck. The truck and engine didn't talk to each other. At one time the doorway between the houses, they told me, was nailed shut. Until somebody with a level head made them undo it. I guess I lasted there six months.

George Schaeffer, Battalion Chief Schaeffer, had a vacancy in Seven Engine. And I asked him, could I go up there. He let me go up to Seven

Engine. He was my Battalion Chief when I was in the Squad. So, I went up to Seven. At least there you got some action. Seven Engine was first due no place. But you caught a lot of action second due behind Twenty and whatever. Then I stayed in Seven a good number of years and Larry Caufield had developed this study group, Freddy Grehl, Larry Caufield, Kossup, and myself. They asked me to change tours so I'd be on the same tour they were.

Then I went to another purgatory. I went to Two Engine which was even worse than Sixteen. Talk about being in the middle of no place. Spend a couple of nights at Two Engine. I think I lasted there about two months. Jimmy Marinucci got promoted to Battalion Chief out of One Engine. I took his place in One Engine which was a nice home. You got enough action there. I had a damn good crew of men. We had a truck company we got along with. I think Iannuzzi was the truck officer at the time. I stayed in One Engine until I got promoted to Battalion Chief.

I always looked forward to the promotions. Given the opportunity, I always wanted to be the boss. I probably don't behave well as a subordinate. (Laughter) I never found any trouble with the transition in rank. When I made Deputy, I remember Dave Kinnear wanted to take training. Joe Redden asked him to pass it over and let me take training because he knew that I was a teacher and that I wanted training. He knew that I wouldn't take it as a transition job; that I would reorganize training and I would do a job for him. So, Dave, the gentleman that Dave is, said, "Yes, sure Ed, I'll take whatever is left." Although he had a lot more seniority than me, Dave stepped down and I became the training boss. And that's where I stayed.

Freeman: I remember when I was studying for my first exam, I studied all by myself. Every once in a while a white guy would come up or a chief and say, "Yes, Rich, study, you'll make it." He may have said, "Here, study this. Study that" But they had groups, study groups then and you were never invited to a study group. None of the black guys, I know were. These guys went to all the communities. They collected all the questions after an exam, right after an exam, and they'd compile a whole group of questions. I got a group of questions from one white guy. Years ago, but that was the extent of it. Everything was hidden.

McGee: Well I started to study. I wasn't much of a studier to be perfectly frank. I never invested in library books like guys did and so on, but one of the fellows from Two Engine who joined the Tact Squad was Jerry Zaccardi. And Jerry and I became friendly and decided to study together a little bit. So we chipped in and bought the Oklahoma set and all that stuff you bought in those days. We studied and we were both fortunate to make captains.

First I was one of those guys who were the temporary captains, one of seven guys. All of us were demoted back to firemen, which was a terrible experience. I was sent from a place I liked, to a place I didn't like. Had to work there for a year and a half, and then get demoted, and sent back to my own company. So it was a very upsetting experience, but you live through it. Then I became a certified captain, for lack of a better word and I went to Fifteen Engine.

It was in the early '70s if I'm not mistaken. Anyway, it was a fairly slow company, but it was one of those companies that after the riots had started picking up as lower income type people started to spread out into the city. You had more fires to go with those localities. So, Fifteen Engine started to pick up, but even when I say slow; it was faster than Seven Engine was when I first went there. So, it was maybe two thousand times, two thousand five hundred times a year when I went to Fifteen. When I left it was probably three thousand, thirty-five hundred. I enjoyed 15 Engine.

Stoffers: The captain's exam, you had a written, a physical, and seniority. The questions on the exam all came out of the Oklahoma series. There was no reading list. You just found a book and read it, hoped that you remembered enough to pass the exam, if the exam came out of that book. But in this captain's exam they did a complete reversal. Before that they were using something else. I don't know what because I never took the exam, but in the captain's exam that I took, it all came out of Oklahoma.

Nobody was studying those books. I had an Oklahoma book there and I would read it. That was because it was light and when it fell down it wouldn't break my nose. And then Tommy Gervel used to come up at night and he'd put the bed light out, take the book and put it on the chair. I think there were something like seven hundred eligible to take the exam. All told the list had thirty-nine people on it when it came out.

The grades on the written were higher than the oral and the seniority. It could have been four, three, and three. It could have been four, four, and two. I don't know. The oral question could have been a disciplinary question. "What would you do if a man did this?" When you first went in, they'd ask you to tell them what you've done so far since you've been on the fire department. That was more a relaxing thing. Get you to talk about yourself. You'd tell them, I was appointed to the fire department at such and such a time and served in such and such a company.

McGrory: I stayed at Seventeen Engine until 1965, when I was promoted to captain. I had started studying a couple of years before that. Captain Wittick got me studying, but I studied mostly on my own. He started me.

He used to type up sheets for us and have drills. They were very extensive sheets on different aspects of firefighting which were very good. In fact, probably still today, I probably still have some of them up in storage. It started me thinking because when I first came on job, they were talking about the forty-two hours coming in. I wasn't eligible to take that exam. That was one of the last of the one liners, true and false. They made quite a few men out of that. The next one I wasn't studying for, I don't know why. But that was when the multiple multiples started. That was a whole other thing. Then I figure, "What am I doing? Let me start." So I started to really study in earnest. I took the next exam and I made it. I came out, oh I don't know, fifth or sixth or something like that.

Miller: I was in Six Truck until 1963. Back then a guy collected the good and welfare and your union dues. He had a little book and he would write your name in it. It looked like a little prayer book and he would sign that you gave him your dues and everything because there was no payroll deductions. There was always an item there called good and welfare. So just out of curiosity, I asked another fireman "What is this good and welfare? Where does it go? What happens to it? I'd like to know." The next day I was transferred to Thirty-two Engine. So I stayed down there about six months until I apologized. But I hadn't done any real serious studying until I got down there. It was so boring that I would study like eight hours a day and that's how I got started studying.

Then I went to Two Truck. And I stayed there for six years until I got promoted to captain. I had been doing a little bit of studying in Six Truck under the tutelage of Dominic LaTorre, who became a captain and then a Battalion Chief after he died. Studying was a lot different in those days. I wasn't a veteran. I was on the job in 1959. In 1960 they had an exam. And the veterans, if you're on the job a year you can take the exam. I did absolutely no studying and for some reason they let me take the exam. They had me down. So I went down and took the exam and I passed it. I think only sixteen guys passed that exam. And I never did any studying. I just went through it.

It was the first type of multiple choice exam they ever had in the city of Newark. It was a, b and c and d or was it c and d or was it b and d or whatever it was. They went down and said, "This guy isn't a veteran." So they threw me off the list. I was just disqualified right off the list. But I didn't know and didn't care. I was only on the job a year. I wasn't qualified to be a captain.

The next exam was 1964. I was eligible for that exam then. And I had been studying, so when the next test came up I was really prepared for it. On that test I came out number thirty-six. I came out fourteenth on the written, but they had a physical at the time. And I was in pretty good shape. I got a ninety physical, but a ninety physical wasn't good enough. Guys were getting ninety-fives and ninety-eights. As a consequence I was left number one on the list. They went to thirty-five guys and I was left number thirty-six.

I did so much time, put so much effort into the written and I didn't into the physical. I figured I'm going to do well against these old timers. I didn't. These guys who just barely pasted the exam, with a ninety-eight physical and seniority jumped ahead of me. So they went to thirty-five guys and I was left number one. I never got promoted off of that list. Giorgio who made captain later, was left number two and he was vice president of the union at the time. He couldn't get promoted, so that was a big mistake, not working out. Some of these guys were in their fifties who got better physicals than I. I learned a lesson. I worked like hell for the physical and then they threw it out for the next exam. I was number three on the next captain's exam. I was promoted in '68.

Dunn: At the beginning of '64 the opportunity came up to take a promotional test. I was in a chief's house and the chief was studying for a promotional test; Captain Griggs studied all the time; and at the same time I became a very close friend of Ed Wall, from working part time with him. As we toured the Bowery in New York talking about the fire department, I found myself more and more interested in studying for the examination. Between Ed Wall, John Griggs, and Chief Nolan, I think I had excellent access to people who had been in the system; had taken tests.

I went home and discussed it with my wife, the effort and the time I would have to put in. We agreed to go for it. I read all the books. I sat down every night in the firehouse and we would study. Whenever I had anything that I had a question on or I wanted some more information, I always had access to probably the best brains in the fire department at that time, between Wall, Griggs, and Chief Nolan. So because of what I'd seen them doing, it gave me a lot of insight into doing the same thing.

When you have a couple of small children in the house though, it is very difficult to study at home. I went to my uncle and said, "Hey, I need a place to study. I can't study in my little four room apartment on Brill Street with two kids, it's very hard." He says "Well, I have a nice apartment on Elizabeth Avenue, five oh five. I'm never home. Come use it any time you want because I'm working days now at Special Service." So I had access to a very private place to study. Every morning I would go, just like I would be going to work. I'd pick up the books I was going to do. I'd have my lesson plan laid out for the day and I'd go to my uncle's apartment. He'd leave me lunch and I would sit there and do my regular five hours of study preparing for the promotional examination.

When the test time came up and I took the test; I found it wasn't a difficult test at all. For some reason as you're preparing for testing you always think they're going to ask you stuff you don't know or they're going to go into deep mathematics and stuff like that. They didn't. They asked logical firefighting questions based on my experience and my reading. I felt I did all right.

That type of test today, they're not using. That was a multiple choice type of test. It was weighed for 6 parts for the written, 2 for seniority, and 2 for a physical. I took the written part. I did very well. I was notified to appear for the physical. I'm not a physical person. When I took the physical it was the same type of physical they used for the entrance test. You had to do so many pushups, so many sit ups, so many squat jumps, climb the rope, jump so many inches. I practiced for that the same as I did for the entrance test. I always felt very good because when the results were in I think I had like the 6th or 7th physical in the fire department. Yet, I wasn't a physical person.

So it shows you if you have to take a math test, you should study math. If you have to do a physical test and the guy tells you "These ten problems we're going to give you." Study those ten problems. I didn't go out and run through the park for nine miles. I didn't join the YMCA. I didn't go to any type of physical program. I didn't do anything different except for what the paper told me I would be required to do. I practiced enough where I could do my thing. So I felt very good.

The promotional list, when it came out, I came out around 16th or 17th on that list. The list moved fairly rapidly.

Carragher: I studied to get promoted. When I think of exams, oral assessments and stuff like that, the first thing I did to study was probably the best thing I could have done to study for an exam today. New York City had a Delahansy Institute and they had a Fire Lieutenant's course over there. I was probably only on the job maybe a year and a half or so and I decided to take this course. It was a correspondence course. I think it was twenty-six lessons. It took me about six months. What it was is you started right off with multiple choice, which is the worst type of questions you could probably do to prepare for a test. But after the first lesson every single lesson you did, you had to write an essay answer. All the tests were corrected by New York City Deputy Chiefs or Chief Officers. They would get down to every scenario, three story frame, a two and a half story house or a church or a shopping center or a mall or a tax payer, anything. You always had to go over a fire from beginning to end. Where would you put your first line? Your second line? Where would you put your other hoselines? Where would you use your truck people? How many people? How many alarms called? Water?

You made a size up, an initial size up, the thirteen-point size up for every single scenario. You went right down the list and did it. At the time I thought I learned a lot from it and I did. From what I see now as a Deputy Chief today, for anyone studying to become an officer on this fire department today, that would be the course to take. When I first came on the job in the Training Academy I bought the Fire Chief's Handbook and I read that cover to cover while I was in the Training Academy. Oklahomas were just becoming popular. I had all the Oklahomas. I had every single fire book that came out. I studied then probably, a slow day of studying, I did eight hours. That was probably five or six days a week, lots of days ten, twelve hours, more studying in the firehouse.

When I went to Twenty Engine or even in the Rescue Squad, I used to study. Then I went to Twenty Engine, they asked, "How can you study here? The house is too busy." But I found time. Come into the firehouse, do your routine in the morning, go up and study for an hour, at night, the same thing. Come in, go up, read. If you get an alarm, come back, go right upstairs again, study again. I disciplined myself. I studied like that probably for a year and a half to two years. And it paid because when I took the captain's exam I came out fifth on my list.

I was made in 1965, August of '65. So I would say, 1963, 1964 I did all my studying because we took the test probably at the end of '64. At the time I had only about three and a half years on the job. I took the test. I only waited a couple of months to be promoted when the list was out because then they promoted according to vacancies. A vacancy came, they promoted you right away.

When I first got promoted I went to Five Engine. That was the only vacancy they had at the time, so they sent me down to Five Engine on the third tour. The Battalion Chief I had at the time was O'Beirne, Chief O'Beirne who later became Chief of Department. He was my Battalion.

I went there as a captain. I was up there thinking, "Well, I'm not staying here. I don't like this house. It's too slow." That was the first day. I went right up to the captain's room, typed out a transfer request because I knew there was a guy retiring in Seven Engine in four weeks. Chief O'Beirne came in. You lined up back then when the chief came into quarters. O'Beirne was the type of chief who questioned you. You read all the general orders in front of him. He would bring in different periodicals he thought were interesting and say, "Cap, I want you to read this to your men." Everybody sat there and you read to them, read the article and you booked everything. But when he walked in the first morning he said, "Cap, is there anything I can do for you." I said, "Yes, sign my transfer request papers." He says, "What? What do you mean? Are you going to give it a shot?" I said, "No, I want to go up on the hill where it's busier." He told me, "You know, if I thought you were leaving here because you didn't like me, I would never sign this. But you don't even know me." I said, "That's right, I don't Chief." He said, "Okay, I'll sign it." He put it through. So, I was there four weeks exactly and then I went up to Seven Engine on the third tour with Harold Davis as my Battalion Chief.

I was only a captain a short while and they had a course, Fire Department Administration, over here in Rutgers Newark. Joe Redden was one of the instructors and Deputy Chief Walsh from New York, who was a retired New York Deputy Chief ran the course. I took that course which was a college semester course. It was a couple of credits, three credits or something like that. I was still reading a little bit, but I wasn't interested too much in taking the Battalion Chief's job at the time. Because I felt, "Jeeze, I'm only a captain a short time." I had two years on the job as a captain when the test came up for Battalion Chief. I took it and again I came out well on it. I think I came out seventh.

They were making chiefs right away. I was I think six or seven one thousandths of a point behind Carl Stoffers. He was promoted the first year the list was out. I waited until the third year. Somewhere prior to the list coming out Vinny Brennen, who was a Battalion Chief in Newark at the time, took a leave of absence to go up to Greenland for eighteen months. He was up there in Greenland and Carl was made. Then there was a vacancy coming up the following month for me. Vinny Brennen came back from Greenland and they gave him the spot. I had to wait two more years to get promoted to Battalion Chief, not until '70. As I said, like six or seven one thousandths of a point behind Carl, one day more of seniority, I would have been promoted before him. One day.

I made Deputy in September of '79. Again, I did some studying for it. Reading the books that were out on the market then and I was lucky also. I just hit the right books for it. In the time I was Battalion Chief, I had another Deputy's exam I took and I didn't come out too well. But I didn't want the job. I was only a Battalion Chief maybe three years or four years and I didn't feel like I was ready to be a Deputy Chief. So, I didn't open a book and it showed because I came out low on the test. Then when it came up in '78, the test was announced in '78. I thought, "Well, I'm going to give it a shot this time. I feel now I have nine years as a Battalion Chief behind me and I can probably do as well as most people." So, I decided then I can read a little bit and I did. I came out well on the test again and got promoted in '79. Went to be a coordinator, we had coordinators there for a short while.

I was coordinator over there in Mount Prospect Avenue, Rescue Squad quarters probably for about eight or nine months and then Jimmy Raymond, who was in the Second Deputy, called me up one day and said that he was going to go to the Arson Squad. Do I think I would be interested in his spot in the Second Deputy? So, naturally I said certainly. So I grabbed the spot. I went down there and stayed until I got bounced up to the First Deputy for a while.

At the time I went down to the Second Deputy we had three battalions in this division, the Second Battalion, the Third Battalion, and the Fifth Battalion. Of course, the Second Battalion has been out a few years now. But you had three battalions and more companies. At the time we still had Four Engine, Two Truck. We had Thirty-Two Engine. We had One Engine. Gradually we lost these. So you can see how we're losing our department real quick. Now you know the first of December in 1994, Deputy Two will be out of service.

Haran: When I was studying everybody was reading books. Four, five guys in the firehouse, he's over here, he's over there. There are a couple of guys studying together. Nobody's going to tell this guy an answer on this because one question may leave you and make him, this type of thing. You had maybe five hundred guys eligible to take a captain's exam and you have maybe, maybe a hundred and fifty guys in the books. And you have another two hundred guys who are going to take the test and hope they get lucky. Which back then, wasn't likely, but it was a possibility. Now out of those hundred and fifty guys who are in the books, you have maybe fifty guys who are really in the books.

What happens is back then they may make thirty, thirty-five guys off the list. But now you have thirty-five guys, the top guys on the list. Not saying that they're the best of the hundred and fifty who were in the books, but you can probably say that fifteen or twenty of them really know what's going on. They really have a good command of the books. They really have a good command of maybe eighty percent of the job. The other guys have a good knowledge of the job because they look in the books. They read the books. They have it. They know something. They know what you're talking about.

I made captain out of the Rescue Squad after putting about eight years in there and went up to Eleven Engine. I stayed there for about a year and a half at Eleven Engine. The opening came in Eleven Truck on the second tour and that's the tour I came off of, those were all the fellows I worked with. As a matter of fact, the day I was promoted there were nine guys promoted. I believe I finished seventh on the captain's list and they promoted nine of us. Bobby Gaynor was the tenth and they didn't promote him that day. They promoted him about three weeks later.

Director Caufield was the director at that time and he called up the first ten men on the list. I happened to work that night. He said, "Ed, this is Director Caufield." I said, "Get the hell out of here." I thought it was Tommy Rush busting me because we were all waiting for the results to come out. So I said, "This is Tommy Rush." He said, "No, this is Director Caufield." I said, "Yeah, yeah." He says, "No, really Eddy, I tell you this is Director Caufield. I just want to let you know that we have the results of the captain's test. I want you to know that you came out number seven. And I just want to congratulate you." He says, "I'm calling up the first ten men on the list to let them know." I'm still skeptical. I don't believe him. It was my first night in the firehouse. Then I believed him. I said, "Okay, Director. Thank you very much. I appreciate this."

But then I got off the phone. All of the sudden other guys got the call. All of the sudden the phone started to ring. "Did you get a phone call from the Director?" Anyhow it was true. I came out seven and the reason I wanted to get back on the second tour was I think the first six men on that list were all guys who we worked with. We were all firemen together off the second tour. It was Jimmy Smith. He came out of Five Truck. We were promoted the same day. Bobby Gaynor, who was number ten, he was working with us, a fireman there. It was me. It was Mike Lawless. Mike Lawless was the other guy. John Higginson, who came out of Four Engine on the second tour. That was five. Lowell Jones, he was number nine. Lowell Jones was number nine. Kingetter was number two or three, I forget. Jimmy Finucan, Jimmy Finucan was number two.

There were ten guys who were promoted. Seven of us all worked together as firemen on the same tour. So, that's why I wanted to get back on the second tour at Eleven Truck. I knew all those guys and I knew all the guys on Eleven Truck were all good guys and good firemen. I wanted to get over there. It turned out, it was a good move for me. They were my best fifteen years on the fire department, Central Avenue. I enjoyed it there. I liked it there.

Cody: I was promoted provisionally, but I still had to take the next exam. I was led to believe that if I didn't get promoted on the next list or come out high enough on the next list, I was going to go back as a fireman, which I didn't want to do. So, I continued to study. And I was fortunate, I come out number seven and I think there were fifteen openings by the time the list came out. So, I just stayed as a Captain. Seven guys were promoted provisionally. Some of them went back, but they all were promoted on that list except for one. It more or less worked out, but it was hard going back. It was hard. I'm sure it was hard for anyone to go back.

We had a multiple choice test with a hundred, a hundred and twenty questions. No physical. At that time everyone studied. It was a big competition. We used to have study groups and meet at each other's homes. We outlined chapters and just continuously made up flash cards and flashed them at one another. There was a lot of knowledge then. A lot of it was never needed and a lot of it was never used, but it was there.

I think the weight on the exam was eight for the written and two for seniority, so seven years, eight years that didn't give me a lot of seniority. I have to give Director Kossup, who was a Battalion Chief at the time, a lot of credit for my studying. I lived across the street from him in Vailsburg on Montrose Street. And I had asked him one time, not knowing much about the job, I asked him if he would help me study if he was going to have a group or something. Before they called for the test, he formed this group and he asked me if I wanted to sit in on it. That's how I ended up provisional Captain, because I ended up thirty-eighth on the list. Not really knowing much at all.

I believe the Battalion Chief's test I took was the last Battalion Chief's test that was a multiple choice exam.

Garrity: When I got promoted I went to Nine Truck. That was January first 1978. That's an interesting story. Chief McLaughlin was the Chief of the Fire Department then. They knew I was going to get promoted. He said to me, "Where do you want to go?" Jimmy Dolon was the Captain in Nine Engine. Getting a truck company when there were only twelve trucks and they're making fifteen guys that day, the odds were that I wasn't going to get a truck because I was the last guy out of the fifteen. I was fifteenth.

So McLaughlin says to me, "Well, where do you want to go?" I said, "If Jimmy Dolon is leaving Nine Engine, I'd go to Nine Engine." He said, "Okay, I'll see what I can do for you." So I got promoted, then I went on vacation. I was on vacation over the holiday. I came back to work. I was assigned to Nine Truck. Well, the first day, like I said we had fires every day, I wasn't in the firehouse two hours. We caught a two bagger on Springfield and Fifteenth and he was there. I said, "Chief, I thought I was going to Nine Engine?" He looks at me. He says, "Nine's a nine. What are you complaining about?" So, that's how I ended up in Nine Truck.

I was assigned there temporarily because Cliff Titcomb was out with a shoulder injury. He was down at the Training Academy. He was supposedly coming back. I was there about four months. Cliff used to stop about once a week to make sure I was running the company right because it was his company and he wanted to make sure I wasn't screwing it up on him. One day he came in and he said, "I'm not coming back. I can't make it." So I filled out transfer papers from roving, temporarily assigned to Nine Truck to permanently assigned to Nine Truck. I was the only one out of the group I was promoted with who got a real assignment. The first fourteen guys were roving. I got an assignment that I stayed in. Everybody said, "Who do you know?" "McLaughlin, he sent me here."

The day I filled out the papers Henny Richter was working. He said, "What, you can't take it here anymore? You're transferring out?" I said, "You didn't read the papers, Henny." He looked at the papers. He said, "You better not do that. Cliff's going to be mad at you." I said, "Cliff just told me he's not coming back." Henny was upset that Cliff was going to be upset at me for putting in for his spot, but when I told him that Cliff said it was all right that I could stay there, then he felt much better about that. So I went there in '78 and I stayed there until May of '89 when I got a provisional promotion to Battalion Chief.

McGovern: I transferred from Twenty-seven Engine to the Rescue Squad and the change was unbelievable. I went from doing my housework and wondering what you're going to have for lunch to going to fires one after the other, just constantly. And in between that trying to keep everything maintained and cleaned. It was a big, big transition. It took me a while to settle into that and at the time I went there, everybody was studying. They had a study group in the house and I was like a pork chop at a Jewish picnic. I was kind of pushed aside because maybe I was would be competition on the test. It was dog eat dog for the captain's test back then. I was naïve. I didn't know what the hell was going on. Eventually, within maybe a month I would say I started being accepted. It was like a test. Once we got the study group going, I was accepted.

It was a like a ritual. After lunch you didn't go to take a nap. It was go upstairs and it was study. We did that for three, four years until everybody I worked with, with one exception, made captain. Why the one guy didn't make it I don't know because he was sharper than everybody. He is just one of those guys who can't take a test. He should have been made a long time ago, but he never was. He wound up retiring as a fireman. But everybody else I ever worked with at the Squad was promoted to either captain or Battalion Chief. My captain retired as a Deputy Chief.

The first Battalion Chief's exam, I took, I came out sixth. I got moved back to ninth and I got left first on the list. Somebody protested a question, moved me back three spots. They made eight. I got left first. That was the first test I took. That was back in '78 or '80 I don't remember the exact year. I took another test and I forget where I came out on that. Anyway, the one I got made off of I came out thirteenth. So they wound up making sixteen or something like that. That was in '96.

The Battalion Chief's test I got made off of was a written and an oral. That was the first oral I took. But the first Battalion Chief's test I took was all multiple-choice, a hundred questions. The one after that I took was all consent decree type oral. That's how that changed.

Prachar: The fire department has lost something because people no longer study. The knowledge men had just from studying will be missed. There was a lot of knowledge. But you had your book knowledge, guys who are book smart, street dumb. Other guys like myself who have street knowledge from the men who taught me when I came on the job. I have the knowledge. Street smarts, book dumb, I'm just not a book man. I can read, but to sit there for hours and hours and hours, days on days, weeks on weeks to study for a test just wasn't my cup of tea.

I know men who gave up working part time, going out with their friends. Years ago we had bowling leagues and softball leagues on this department, gave that up to study and study. Then take the test and come out thirtieth. Guys wanted to hang themselves. I know wives who wanted their husbands out of the house almost to the point of divorce because they were so obsessed with studying to get promoted. But at the same time, that guy who was studying so much, he forgot his street smarts. He became such a book man that when you went to teach guys in the firehouse how to do things, it was strictly by the book. The guy who had street sense, could explain stuff more to the person coming on. "This is an axe." Where in the book, "This is a handle, a piece of metal and it forms an axe." Teach me the basics. Let me learn the basics.

You do need the book people. There's no doubt about it. You need those people. You need that system brought back because there's a lot of knowledge that those people have that can't be passed on to you just by street smarts. To run into a chemical building, which when you're studying you had to know your chemicals, these guys would say, "Stop, think of where you're going. What do we have in here?" Where years ago you just went in and did that job. Let's think now. Can this go through the skin? Can it be an irritant? Book knowledge, where somebody with street knowledge would just go in and, God forbid, get killed. You do need that book knowledge, certain parts of it.

You didn't need guys spending weeks, months on end, never come out of a room in the firehouse because they had to have that promotion. I have to be number one. I can't be number two on this test because they may not go to number two, so I have to be number one. I put up with one man for years. The Battalion Chief's test was coming up. Had to have it. Had to have it. Come out after the exam. "How'd you do?" "I blew two questions.

Cost me my promotion." Talk to his wife. "Call him up. Let's go out. Let's do this. Just to get him away from these God damned books." Nope, got to study. Got to study. It affects you mind after a while, but you do need people like that, book men.

I also feel you need people like me with the street sense. Like I said, street sense I've got. I taught a couple of kids on this job. How I do it my way. Why my way? Because I feel it's street smarts. I may not be able to do it the way the book says. There's two ways to fight a fire. There's a book's way and there's a fireman's way. If you don't know the fireman's way, you get out the book knowledge. Book knowledge you can keep. Book knowledge can be passed on, but street smarts can only be learned.

The testing back then was the proper way, still is the proper way. You always get that one or two guys who shouldn't be a leader who will be, but eventually they can weed them out to other positions where they can't hurt anybody. I wouldn't want it on my conscience that some guy was sick or seriously injured or died, heaven forbid, because I didn't do something. That I didn't see something that he was doing and stop it right in the bud. That's the difference between your old day testing and today's testing. You had officers then. Some of your officers now are not officers. I'm an officer a year and a half, but I don't consider myself really an officer because I haven't hit my plateau.

I did hit my peak a couple of times as a fireman because I felt as far as my knowledge was concerned; I was where a fireman should be. That all came from my officers; not only my captain, but my Battalion and my Deputy.

McDonnell: I studied ten times as much as I studied to graduate from college to get promoted to captain. That's no exaggeration. I studied five, six hours a day for five years. Jimmy Smith used to study eight hours a day. He used to study with a stop watch. If he studied six hours today, tomorrow he had to do ten. At your change of tours guys were trying to stump you. Ask you questions. Guys were going, taking exams and writing the questions down. I would make up my own tests on everything. Hand them around.

T. Grehl: I read everything I possibly could and obviously my father helped me because my father was very much a student all through his time on the job. So, he basically tutored me, told me what to read, what to do. e still had his contacts, so once a month we would meet with a guy who became a Deputy Chief over in Paterson or Passaic. I forget. Chief Galliger from the Irvington Fire Department who wound up becoming the chief of the department, my father tutored him. I spent one night every other week over at his house in Irvington studying.

Myself, Mike Ruane, and Warren Bongo actually started together studying. Warren decided he didn't want to take the test to get promoted, but Mike and I still studied. We studied for a long time and I gave up a lot. I still remember seven days a week, five, six hours a day studying, not going out with my wife and then the test was cancelled. I don't remember why. But the test was cancelled. Then it was held in another eight or nine months after that.

We studied everything. We studied all the IFSTAs, The Fire Chief's Handbook, several management books, the NFPA which was like three times the size of a Bible, trying to remember all that, recording it on tapes. We had at least a hundred old exams at our disposal. We studied and memorized any old question from an exam we knew of. We'd listen to tapes we recorded. We put a lot, a lot of time in because it was very, very competitive. One question, two questions could mean the difference of twenty spots at the time. In fact, I just gave the copy of our results to Chief Jones because he came off that test. He was like three or four and I was like fourteen. I found the old copy in my locker, who had how many right and wrong and the seniority. So I sent it up to him.

Yes, it was very, very competitive. There were a lot of books to study and they didn't tell you what books either. That was the worst part. Like a couple of tests ago, at least they told you these ten books are going to be on it. But back then they didn't. If Civil Service had given a test in Paterson the year before and decided that Joe Blow was the author and they used one question of his, everybody went out and bought the book because they might use another one. If Harry Carter wrote a book and they used one question out of his, everybody bought that book. We just bought every book. It wasn't that they told you these five books, six books. You knew that the Oklahomas at the time, they weren't called the IFSTAs then, would always be on. The Fire Chief's Handbook would always be on. There were certain books you always knew, but you just read whatever you could and obtained whatever you could. It was a long process at the time.

People who were in study groups wouldn't talk to other people. If people walked in the room they would close their information. You could work with them. If you were in different study groups you weren't even talking about it. We took a lot of tests for practice too. If there was a test given for some dopey inspector in Hackettstown, we took it because there might be one or two questions they would answer for the captain's test a year later. There was a lot of preparation, a lot of time.

Ryan: Captain's test was very interesting. It was the assessment center type thing. Again, took many courses. If this is the only game in town, I'm going out and playing. If it's left handed hook shoots, I'm going to practice like mad. Knew the format of the test. What it was going to be. Studied for that. Practiced, practiced, and practiced. Worked out. If a person is determined to advance himself, no matter what constraints are put upon them or what field they're playing on, if they practice and work at it and understand the testing process, they will succeed at it. That's just a matter of determination. Whether it's a multi-choice question test which would entail memorizing a whole bunch of stuff or a role playing type model, you still have to know your stuff. Basically you have to know all the other training stuff, but you have to be able to interact with people. That's what that brought out.

Chief's test, I thought I did horrible. I did. I worked so hard at that. I really wanted it bad and I worked so hard. I came out of there and I gave out a big yell because I knew the one part I had goofed up. I only got a four on that out of five. As it turned out, it worked out well. But I did well enough.

The things is, whatever field you're studying, whatever the test is, whatever it's going to be, you have to work at it. Until you have it down pat and they can't throw you any curves. If you get a perfect score, what are you going to do? If you know it, if you've been into it, you know when you goofed up. That's why I hollered at myself because I felt bad about it. So, I only got a four out of five in one of the sections.

That's another thing that's changed dramatically. When I first came on we would study a good three, four hours a day. An alarm would come in, okay, close the book, put it down, come back, clean up, back to the reading, studying, had your nose propped in a book. In any firehouse you went into, there were guys with their noses stuck in a book. You got a lot of knowledge, you really did. A lot of it was not applicable, but you didn't know. You picked up on it. You became a student of the job. I don't know how the personality type testing that they're doing now is going to work out. Not too many people read books. Books, I think, are a necessity.

Actually, what's probably more critical now is a constant implementation of training at the Training Academy to fill that void. Where people had to study all the books and learn all the options and tactics and strategies to make captain, now they have to learn it at the Academy. Because if you wanted to get promoted, previously you had to study the books. Virtually memorize, God knows how many books, thirty books. And I'm not talking little books, big ones, true students of the job. I don't see that anymore. I really don't.

Carter: My class, the first class in '73 in the new academy, had a beautiful opportunity. The Battalion Chief who was the executive at the time under Ed Wall, who was commandant, was Jim Morgan. He told us all to start studying because "You're all veterans and under civil service you can take the test first shot and it's coming up in about a year or two." Well, I had been studying in Rahway and I had been a fireman in the Air Force where you had to study. They made you read the books all the time. So, I figure what an opportunity.

Now in Eleven Engine up on the second floor there was a small room where the repeater for the fire department was located. I had a chair in that room and I just sat in there hour after hour. Everybody is downstairs celebrating the three hundred sixty five days of Saint Patrick's Day and I'm up there studying. I really poured my heart and soul into it. The test was scheduled originally in '76 when they had the layoffs. This was back in the days when everybody studied, whether you were thought you had a chance or not you studied because you might just hit it lucky. Well, everybody got the bad spirit. Nobody touched a book for three or four months. Finally I said, "What's up here? You're a real asshole if you don't study." You never know. They could like stutter step and hold it a year later. Well, the test did come out in February of '77.

In the old days we had a real game. I mean study groups. Guys getting together to pour over the books, make up questions, try and dissect the book to see what was the best way to remember. It usually broke out to rote learning. To this day, I use Fried's size-up from Fire Ground tactics and I memorized it in Eleven Engine. I had everything on a card. I memorized it by the first letter of each word because in the old days if you didn't have it on the tip of your tongue and right in the front of your brain, you were going to be a fireman for a long time.

After we took the exam, we would go down to review our answers. They would show you a corrected exam and we would compile lists of questions and answers used on tests. So, you could trade for other towns and stay current on what the questions were. The civil service had a terrible tendency not to change their questions. They'd just put the front of the question in the back and the back in the front and put it out again. I was down there and counted twenty-two wrong as I sat looking at my paper. I was taking notes as best I could on the questions. I came out of the room and Joe Pierce was a captain at the time studying for Battalion Chief and he said to me, "Harry, how many did you get wrong?" I said, "I guess twenty-two it looks like."

In those days as you thought about it, your mind started to cloud over, you'd say twenty-two, maybe twenty-three. Maybe outside twenty-five. Well the list comes out in May of '77 and I came out number twelve with less than four years on the job, zero seniority practically. When I figured up the grade it worked out to twenty-two wrong. It just shows you your first impression is usually the best impression. They made nine captains real quick.

The thing that impressed me about the whole deal at the time was that the Director called the first twenty guys on the list personally to congratulate them. Many people tell many stories about John Caufield, but now that he's gone the thing that I miss about him most is that he was a gentleman. He really got a thrill out of promoting people. When you did something, he really got a thrill. You don't make enemies. You make friends. I was in the National Guard. He tracked me down on active duty and I get the phone call. "Congratulations Harry, you're number twelve." I had gotten my card anyway in the mail. It just happened to come that morning. Although I was happy to get the official thank you from him, when I got my card out of my Post Office box and our Post Office in Adelphia then was in the old firehouse, I was so excited, I went screaming off. I went and hit the panic bar door and put both hands into the glass window and knocked the safety glass from its frame, blew the front door window right out of the firehouse. Everybody was, "What the hell happened to him? He was mumbling. He was screaming, 'Twelve, twelve, twelve' as he ran out of the firehouse."

Anyway, I get promoted. I waited all through the summer, the longest summer of my life. Guys who waited years and years and years think I'm a real, real wimp for saying I had to wait six months to get promoted. Longest six months of my life, I get promoted on the eleventh, effective the fourteenth of November, 1977. The day I was promoted, Chief Morgan from Training was promoted from Battalion to Deputy and I was promoted from fireman to captain, two of us in the room, two families, two people celebrating.

Deal maker that I tried to be, I had been a ticket buyer for the John Caufield Association for a while, so I contacted a friend of mine up in the

Bureau. Sam Synicki and said, "Hey, what can you do? I got a duke. I'd like to stay on the first tour and Frank Lipere is moving out. There's an opening down at Fifteen." "Fifteen Engine, Tour One. No problem." He writes it down. Gives it to the Director's secretary, Ester Conrad and they lost it. They lost it. So the day I get promoted, I'm expecting to go to Park Avenue with Louie Formisano the chief and they announce, "Okay, Carter, you're going to Eighteen on the Third Tour."

Well, Avon Avenue, you might as well be assigned to a deathless, wasteland somewhere because they were losing about a battery a night over there. The neighbors were robbing them blind. So, I went over there scared to death. I didn't know anything about Chief Carragher, who proved at the time to be a decent guy, but I was there from November of '77 when I got promoted to January of '78 when I finally got Louie Formisano and Jim Moony to get the Director's ear and get me where I was supposed to be. Then I went to work on Park Avenue.

Langenbach: Probably before the layoffs, I just started reading. I was in a house with George Daudelin and Tommy McDonnell who were both studying heavy. They said, "This is what we're doing." I went to a fellow in Bloomfield and bought all the books, the IFSTAs, and started reading, the IFSTA ladder book, the IFSTA engine book, and The Fire Chief's Handbook. I still have my first Fire Chief's handbook. I started studying. I took the first exam. I can't remember what year that was. I was like eighty-sixth. I think I finished eighty-sixth and they made fifty guys. Then I got serious the next time. That's one of the reasons I jumped over to the engine, because I wanted to get ready just in case it happened. That was the old question and answer exam.

When I got serious about it, I studied every day a couple of hours a day. Twelve Engine in the bunkroom had what they called the iron room. It was a bunch of lockers facing one way so it made a room, a separate room. I used to go in there and just lock myself in there and read and read and read and read. I picked up from Tommy and George, they made flash cards with questions. So every time I read a chapter, I'd underline whatever I wanted to underline and then go back and make questions out of it. Make little flash cards, where ever I was I had my stack of flash cards with me. So, I could keep reading. Like how many feet of ladders are on a class one ladder truck and things like that, according to the NFPA, according to whatever. So, that's what I did over and over and over again. Yes, it was serious business.

I ran into Chief Buccine at a racket. The Chief had just made Battalion Chief and we were shooting pool, a real nice guy, Bob Buccine. And I said, "Chief, what do you do part time?" He said, "I study. That's the only way you're going to get any money around here. You've got to study." And that's what he did. Studied for every exam. That was kind of like an inspiration, too. But yes once I got into it, I hit it real hard. Anybody who really wanted to get promoted, that's what you did. You just kept studying and studying and studying and reading.

I was promoted to captain in July of '82. The test I took was the old multiple choice test. That was the last multiple choice test that counted. There was one after that one and they threw it out. Then they went to the new version of whatever they're doing. My Battalion Chief's test was an assessment center.

Once I got into the books I stayed even though the Battalion Chief exam was an assessment center. I stayed with the same books. Kept in the books. I never went to any of those Bernstien or PASS or Score, or any of those other things. No, I went strictly with what I knew. I moved it up a notch and started looking at the management, leadership, and all that other stuff. So that's how I studied for them. I didn't go to acting school.

Connell: The first test I took was approximately eighteen months after I came on the job. I finished a hundred and seventy-eighth. At that time the NFPA was the fourteenth edition. I believe we're up to the eighteenth edition now. Then there was The Fire Chief's Handbook, Clarke's Principle Practices, Casey's Handbook on Hydraulics, and the whole Oklahoma series. The two hundred series wasn't out then. It's one through ten for basically what the two hundred series is now. Then you had the three hundred series. That was management. Four hundred series, I can't remember what that was about. But the three hundred series was four books and the four hundred series, I think it was five books. The one hundred series was ten books. The two hundred series had about twelve books and it was two or three out of there you had to study. But basically you had to lay out at least three to four hundred dollars for the books to read. And you had to put a heavy time commitment into the studying of it.

The second test I came out, I think I was twenty-seventh, twenty-eighth, somewhere in there. I was in the high twenties. For that, two years before the test, I committed from seven to nine-thirty every night to studying. Three hundred sixty-five days a year including Christmas, New Years and everything else. When I was at work or I was home, made no difference. At that time they had Wometco. It was like a paid channel that was piped into your house. I bought that for my wife to occupy her and my daughter while I was studying because I didn't want to be bothered.

I gave up from seven to nine-thirty seven days a week for two years just studying. I spent one whole year on the fourteenth edition of the NFPA, which is a monster to read. At the end of the year I spent in that I could almost tell you the page number and whereabouts on the page of anything you wanted to know about fire. I had it down pat and that was my key to passing that test. There were fifty-five questions on the captain's test I took from the NFPA and I got fifty-three out of fifty-five correct. The rest were taken from The Fire Chief's Handbook, the Oklahoma series. McNiff just came out with his book, and the rest were coming out of his book. But you had a list of maybe twelve to fourteen books the test was based on. They tell you nothing. What the test was going to be on. It was going to be here. You get a hundred questions and the best scores out of a hundred would be made captain. It was up to you to put the time, the effort, and the money into doing it. The fire department officers and even the firefighters were a lot more knowledgeable about the hazards involved in fire and the different techniques of fighting fire than they are today.

I was on the job a little bit over eight years when I got promoted. That was in '82. It was the last list of the old style testing. The next test they had they threw out in court saying it was not fair to minority firefighters due to terminology or whatever. They started more or less another test, which they had a little argument with and they went through this assessment center garbage they have now.

When I was studying for Battalion Chief, they came out with a book list. I was doing that. There are schools out there that teach you how to be a great actor, but I was torn between promotion and retirement so I figured I'd try it on my own. So I bought one book, Oral Assessment Centers. Read that. I went to the test. The first part of the test was a practical, which was the first time they did that in about eight years. That surprised me. I did very well on that. Then came the scenario part, which I did so-so on. That was it. The list came out. My seniority pulled me through. I came out number seven on the list. Ultimately decided to stay on the job and become a Battalion Chief instead of retire.

There was a wait before they promoted me. They had me dancing on a string for a little bit over a year. But doing that they more or less cemented that there will be no extensions and I will leave with thirty years or less. They kept on saying next month. As a matter of fact, they called me up, told me to report there one day in December. I went there with my wife and family and they asked me what I was doing there. I said, "I was supposed to get promoted today." They said, "Nobody told you it was cancelled?" So, I said, "No, not as of now, but now I know so we'll go home."

Perdon: The first test, all the answers had to be qualified. It was a multiple choice. That was it. It had a bibliography that was as long as your arm. You were afraid not to read books. You read everything. If there was a rumor that they might have a book on the test, you read it. I hit all the seminars because you were afraid not to. It paid off. They didn't move on that test, but I was high on the list. But the next one around was when they started going to the assessment center. They still didn't have their scoring down. That's when they went from fifty-fifty down to pass or fail. That was on the written. They ranked you off the assessment. So, I started off with the written. Without even doing anything, I was in the top twenties there. Once they made that written part pass or fail and they went all assessment center; I went to eighty. I actually got left number two. They promoted seventy-eight guys and left me number two.

I got promoted off the next one. That third time around with the assessment center, I went to a couple of classes. I went to Bernstien, that type of class and just practiced with other people who were taking the test, the assessment part. It paid off. They made it a joke. They made a joke out of the test.

Ricca: First captain's list, I studied with Teddy Holod, God rest his soul. Night and day, day and night at his house and my house. On the back porch at my house with the ceiling fan going like I'll never forget it. We're out there drinking sodas, studying. We'd study until ten, eleven o'clock then go Down Neck to have a little bit to eat. I'd drop him off at Five Truck for the rest of the night. I'd go home. The list comes out. He's nineteen. I'm twenty. Couldn't have happened better unless we came out one and two. But Teddy was elated. He was the push I needed.

Pat Tansey doesn't realize, but Pat made a statement once that helped me. I had mentioned one time about studying. He said, "What are you just afraid you're not going to do as well as your brothers?" He said, "Just do it." It was a boost that I needed. To this day I really owe him a thank you.

Then the quotas rumors came out, that they're going to make one and five. So, I'm theoretically twenty-five now. They asked the first twenty-five guys, to kick in a thousand dollars to push for the quota. I start getting calls, "You're a scum bag. You're this and that." I never donated. I never kicked in and there was one other fellow who didn't and that was Calvin Jackson, who to this day I tip my hat to because he would have been promoted as a minority fireman.

So, we're going to meetings. "You twenty-five guys suck." This and that. I said, "Whoa, I didn't even donate." But my name got put in the ring. Well, the long and the short of it came. They think they're going to make thirty guys now. So, now the next five guys were calling me. "Where do I write the check? Who do I write it out to?" From then on I realized it's not a "we" department. It's an "I" department and it was every man out for himself. I just felt I made it on my merit. I deserved it and just said, "Whatever happens, happens." But I wouldn't contribute. That was the list they threw out.

I prepared for the next test by going to Fire Edcon. I went to the different courses. I practiced with a video camera of myself being interviewed. I read whatever supervision book I could get my hands on. I had one book that was from I.T. & T. for their supervisors. I read that and I figured that the bigger companies were the first to come out with a lot of these new methods, not that they're new methods of supervision, a little bit more of hands on supervision. I read a Post Office book that they gave out. My biggest thing was acting, acting in front of the TV set and being comfortable talking with somebody, nothing to do with firefighting

I still read the IFSTAs and Fire Chief's Handbook. You see when I studied the first time, I put everything on index cards. So, I have about five thousand index cards. What I would do is take a book, a whole pack of cards was one book, leave them in the car and flash card myself. I had the firematics down. It was the acting that I didn't have down and basically that's what it came down to. God rest his soul, Frank McCrone topped that list and Frank had a good bellowing speaking voice. He was a radio announcer for Seton Hall. Firematics though, I don't think he picked up a book. Nothing bad against him at all, but for him to come out number one on the test, a captain's test, without having any firematic background from the books, was unheard of.

He was at Five Truck. I'm sure he went to a million fires, but guys would laugh about it. Guys would say, "I didn't do anything. I went to the Fire Edcon course." They had the one course. We were in the Holiday Inn. They filmed us. That was the one thing guys went to. It was a three hundred dollar course. Three hundred bucks and you're a captain. The guys like Teddy Holod, Phil Cardillo, and Mickey Martino. Guys who should have been captains years ago, but had a problem, couldn't take a test. Rocco Pegaro used to call up Five Truck when those guys were studying and fire answers back at them. Rocco sat down at a test. Rocco blew it. Guy would have probably made the best captain in the world. That's what ended up happening. You lost the cream of the crop.

But the demise of the multiple choice firematics type of exam was the ruination of the department. Ruination of the department because before, if you failed a test, you still studied for two years. So you still had something up in your head. Now, you don't have to study and if you fail it, you wait until the next time and act again. Act two, act three, but before even if you didn't pass, you still studied. Everybody read. There wasn't a guy who didn't walk around with a book. Sure you may have gotten like a Joe Lefchak. Joe just never wanted it. But there's a guy who would have been a super captain.

It really took the wind out of my sails. My aspirations were to become a Deputy Chief on this job, not just become a captain. I had a family tradition. Chief Mike put it one day at Twelve Engine kitchen. He said, "Deputy, Battalion, and Dopey." That was the way he labeled us. Anyway, I made fun of his hair and six months later mine all fell out. Most guys took this job to become a Deputy Chief. They didn't take the job just to be fireman their whole career. My brother Angelo was the youngest captain, youngest Battalion, youngest Deputy, and the first Italian Deputy Chief in the city of Newark, but things ran right for him. He was a good studier and things were right in a row for him, almost like they were made for him. I've taken one captain's test and two chief's tests in twenty-six years when it's supposed to be every three years.

Gesualdo: Basically did probably what everybody else did to prepare for the captain's test. You go home. You don't really get very much done. You've got young kids. You've got soccer. You've got baseball. You've got ballet. Came to the firehouse and just put myself in a corner. My captain used to let me use his room and I read whatever I thought was pertinent, Fire Chief's Handbook. I went to seminars, quite a few seminars, but not for captain, I didn't go to any promotional classes. I just pretty much did it on the reading thing and study groups. Charlie, myself, Don just sat there at nights sometimes firing questions at each other.

I think the exam I was promoted from was the first one they had given with the oral part. Where you had to do the scenario, size up and all that. I don't remember if the first captain's test I took had that. I don't think it did. That was the one they threw out anyway, so apparently it didn't. This was the first one that they actually had the scenario part where you had to give a size-up and an oral part of the exam. That was pretty hard to do because you really didn't know how to prepare for that. That was just kind of like wing it, adlib, but apparently I did all right.

Chapter Five: Adjusting to Promotion

Redden: After you get promoted, now instead of being responsible for what you yourself did and a one point operation at a fire, now you're responsible for a crew of men, their well-being, for an apparatus, and all the equipment and the firehouse. At a fire, determining where to stretch line; of course that changes whether you're first due, second due, or what have you. Checking on the men, you would be on the line. Usually, it's the captain and at that time two men, stretching in a two and a half inch line. You'd be with them. You'd have a man outside at the pump and then possibly, if you were riding pretty good, you'd have an extra man. You'd relieve guys if you were taking a beating. But again there was a family deal where you were just responsible for the well-being of your men and making decisions at fires as how to best handle the situation. At the same time don't get your men into situations where they're going to get injured or something like that.

It wasn't a difficult transition for me. Again because I did have the experience of driving the chief and seeing companies operate. When I was driving the chief, too, I used to seek out some of the fellows who I considered to be the better captains. I used to talk to them and ask them about how they operated. Many of them were good. They gave me a lot of good advice.

After I passed the Battalion Chief's test, I guess I was appointed within a year after the list came out. I was assigned to the Second Battalion on Mulberry and Lafayette Street. Well of course the Second Battalion had the whole downtown area, the high value district up to High Street. It was an interesting battalion. I enjoyed it thoroughly. You had Elizabeth Avenue. You had Frelinghuysen Avenue. You had industry and you had the high rises. In between you had neighborhoods that were starting to deteriorate down around Ten Engine in that area. So, you had a good mixture of just about everything that you would run into in the fire department. For the time I was there, I enjoyed it.

My responsibilities shifted as a Battalion Chief. You're in charge of a whole district, a number of companies. You have to make sure they train and at that time, that they got out and inspected because they did have radios. Tactically at a fire, most times, you had to make the initial decision as to how to approach the fire. What the one problem is that has to be handled immediately, whether it was life hazard or if there's no life hazard, the extension of the fire. If you don't have either one of them, you can knock the fire down quickly. You have to make sure that the men are operating in safe conditions.

You go around to the firehouses in your battalion and inspect to make sure the equipment is in good shape; that the houses are in good shape, being kept up. Of course that was a problem with four tours. If you go into a situation where you have a problem as far as maintenance of the rig or maintenance of the house and you jump all over your captain, he has three other guys who should be doing the job, too. That made it very difficult.

As the Second Deputy I had the Fifth Battalion and the Second Battalion. So, now you have effectively about a third of the city that you're responsible for and essentially you do this working through two Battalion Chiefs. You have to make sure that they're on the ball. That they're doing the job in their battalion as far as training and the welfare of the men, up keep of the apparatus, making sure that they're running a good inspection program. Also that they know what they're doing when they get to a fire and of course ultimately, how they handle a fire situation. Because the Battalion Chief is the one who starts out the operation in most instances. You know the first due engine company will get there and the captain will have to make a quick size-up and determine where to go. But then the

Battalion Chief is the one who comes and he determines essentially how the fire is going to be fought. So, you have to have a lot of confidence and you have to be able to know that he knows what he's doing at a fire, particularly, from the standpoint of effectively handling the fire and protecting the men from possible injury.

There was more paper work as a Deputy. You had to go in once a day and pay a visit to the Chief. Most times that was only a BS session, but what I used to do was I would visit the various companies. I would let the Battalion Chief know, "I'm going to be in your district today." I would go in and eyeball the house, the apparatus, and the men. I might take a look at the house watch book to see how they were. If I saw something that should be corrected, I would speak to the Battalion Chief and tell him that, "I saw this, this, and this." And I would want this done. No problem. I had good Battalion Chiefs working for me.

When I got to the fire, I would want the Battalion Chief to report to me to let me know what was going on; how he sized-up the situation; and what he was trying to do. If I had to make any changes to it, I would make it and then I would send him to the most critical part of the operation. Whether it was a lifesaving operation or whether we wanted to cut the fire off, the Battalion Chief would be assigned to that area, the critical problem that we had to handle. Once the critical problem is handled, the fire is out as far as I'm concerned. We would get together when the fire was knocked down to determine who we're going to hold and what had to be done as far as overhaul is concerned. Then I would take up.

I came out first on the Fire Chief's list and I was a veteran and I think Joe Drew and Jimmy Gaynor were the next two. They were non-veterans. So, I had to be made or nobody was made. If Joe Drew was a veteran, I believe he would have been made. This was just at the time when they were having an election. Carlin was the mayor and Addonizio was running against him.

After Addonizio won, they told me they couldn't promote me to Chief because they were a lame duck administration. There was some kind of law where you couldn't appoint anybody. But in my case it was not an appointment. It was for promotion. But I figured I wasn't going to fight them because they're going to have to give it to me eventually and if I stayed until the bitter end I'd be Chief twenty-six years. So, I'm not going to worry about a couple of months. Then Addonizio became mayor and they promoted me to Chief around July sixth of '62.

F. Grehl: As you went up the ranks, people don't realize the amount of activities you have to think of and the amount of factors you have to consider, the weather, how hard the men have worked, the equipment they have, the man power that's there. You have to put all these things together. You say, "Oh, my God. This is the fourth fire for these guys. I have ten minutes work out of them, twenty at the very, very most. I have to get help." These are the kind of things you have to think about.

Masterson: When you become a captain, there's a change. You're responsible. You've got to know who you're dealing with. You're not dealing with a bunch of kids who are just coming into the Army at seventeen, eighteen years old. You're dealing with guys who are fathers and grandfathers. They're all mature men. Treat them as they are, like you're just talking to them. You don't run around charged with orders and all this kind of crap. Demanding this or that, they know. All men on the fire department, they know what's got to be done. Maybe you just mention, "We've got to get this done today." not in an order way. Orders get you nowhere because then after a while, they'll just sit there and not do anything unless they get an order.

So, you have to try to get an even flow. In other words, to see that things are being done without hollering at everybody to do it. Because you've got to find some way to get it all done, otherwise when you're a fireman, you sit there and wait for them to tell you. And then you have to look at all the windows, well they don't look that bad, to hell with it, we'll skip them. But if they don't look that good, you know somebody better get the windows today, just the front ones. Nobody will see the back windows, something like that. But you've got to work with them. You need them. Without them you're nothing, without the men you're nothing. You're nothing. A captain? What do you think, he puts the fires out? A captain doesn't put out any fires.

McGee: It was a different experience as a captain because you at least had an opportunity to be responsible instead of letting somebody else make the decisions. I had worked in types of companies that afforded me the experience to be a pretty good captain. And I was very fortunate to always have good men working with me. So, it was easy to be the captain in most places I went.

At first I was nervous to be the captain because it is a responsibility. Also I was surprised at some of the responses from some people I had known for years. That weren't as welcoming as I would have hoped. And yet I was also happy by some of the responses of some of the new guys who I went to be the captain of. Who really cooperated with me a thousand percent. So it made my job completely easy.

I never had any really serious disciple problems. If I did they were usually attached to some person's medical condition like drinking or drugs or something, which really was something that couldn't be addressed by me. But in terms of personnel problems with likes or dislikes and things like that, not too much.

I was very fortunate and very happy that it turned out that way. But there were certain people, I don't want to use the word jealous, but I used to say, "Jeeze, that's more proof. If a guy like me can do it, you can do it." I was very happy to get it. It was good for my kids, not so much for me. It's good to be able to tell your kids you're a captain. Really, not that it's a big deal, but it is a big deal in that respect.

Other than that, it didn't change me very much other than I used to think a little bit more. I started to really discuss and try to learn from guys who I had respect for. What I should do in this situation or that situation. I got some really good advice from some guys and I took it. I tried to teach. Even today, I get phone calls now and I'm out five years. Just as late as a month ago, a fireman called me to tell me how much he appreciated what I had taught him in the fire department. So, I consider myself a little bit of a teacher. I tried to teach guys that driving the engine meant more than just steering the thing toward the fire. It meant knowing the apparatus. It meant knowing how to make the hook ups and gauge the pressures and so on and so forth. Guys appreciated that and I enjoyed doing it, so it was a complimentary thing.

Denvir: I went from a truck company to an engine company when I made captain. So it was more of a change than just rank. On a truck company you're running free. You're by yourself a lot. You know where your partners are. You try to stick together, but the captain really just has to trust you and you have to trust him. Know you have these certain jobs to do and just do them. He's not there to direct you. He has his functions to do.

Things he has to do. He's like a working supervisor. He's just in charge. In an engine company, basically you're sticking together. You're stretching line together. Your objectives at the fire are two different things. One is search, ventilation, and rescue. The other is drown it, get the fire out. The quickest way you can.

I found the transition was easy. In a truck company you don't get to use a line much. There's a lot of excitement and enjoyment working with the lines. In the truck you do a lot of work. You work hard. There are going to be so many things to do. You go from one thing to the other. Ventilation and overhaul, you raise ladders first. Then whatever you have to do. There are a lot of things for a truckman to do. I like both ways, but I preferred the engine, I think, especially as an officer.

Freda: I was at Fifteen Engine for approximately four or five years. Then I got promoted to captain and from there I was transferred to Engine Company Twelve which is a big transfer for me because I was a fairly young firefighter. I came from a very slow firehouse and I was transferred to one of the busiest firehouses in the city or maybe the busiest in the city at that time. The second hurtle that I had to overcome was that the people who I would command were much older than me. So it was more or less a shock, me being assigned there. I really learned to be a firefighter there, even though I was on the job for several years. I think the supervisory training became very good there because they were all older men. Some of them had fifteen years' experience on me.

I had two things to overcome. First was the difference in experience. Second was the difference in the houses themselves. When I went to Twelve Engine it was like going to a different world. The housework wasn't done. The house is situated in the ghetto. Possibly, psychologically you became part of the ghetto. The house looked like the ghetto. There was one bathroom in the place with one toilet hole and one sink to service the Salvage Company and Twelve Engine. So, the whole atmosphere of the place is tense for people who want to be clean.

I think I had an impact on changing it because before I came there I heard horror stories. That sort of scared me as a young kid. When I first went there every window in the place had been broken. It almost looked like a scene from World War II where they had the black outs. I couldn't understand what happened until I later found out that beer cans had been thrown through every window in the firehouse. Not on this tour I was on, but other tours. These are the things you had to contend with.

There were a couple of captains there who would engage in arguments. They would engage in arguments after a few drinks on how to pull a ceiling. They would literally go get a hook and pull the ceiling in the kitchen. You'd come in and find plaster all over or you'd find the front door of the firehouse forced open because of an argument on how to open a door. Now how do you handle these situations? I didn't know. They just existed. They were all tough guys. They were all bigger than me. They would have fought me in a minute. I probably would have had to call the police. So, they just existed until these men retired or I left.

That was a tremendous change in not only dealing with my own men, but dealing with the other men on the other tours and the officers on the other tours. It was a tremendous challenge for a fairly young man who was just appointed captain and came from a very slow company being thrown into this.

After I was promoted to Battalion Chief, I roved for about three years. And it was really an eye opener because I roved in every battalion. See, it came at a time when Battalion Chief rovers weren't on certain tours. In those days you used to cover four tours. When you got a call to fill in a roving assignment, it could have been to tour one, two, three, or four in any battalion. At first it was a pain in the neck because you always had a bag with your rubber goods and your bedding and anything else you wanted. You would literally carry it around from site to site. Sometimes it was for two weeks, sometimes for two days, and other times it would be one day or one night and you'd be lugging your stuff around with you.

It was a very interesting experience because you really got a total view of firefighting, not only in the different battalions, but on different tours. A lot of it was different than your concepts, because you came from a certain battalion, and it would change from tour to tour. It would change not only in firefighting strategy. But it would change from discipline. It would change with respect for officers and the firefighting strategy definitely changed.

I think it was mostly caused by the officers. I don't blame too much on firefighters. I always found the toughest firefighter around, the one who sits around and tries to be the toughest; when he knew you wanted something done, you made it mandatory, they may gripe, but they would do it. I think a lot of officers didn't demand too much or fell into their life style.

I'll give you one example. I was roving in the Second Battalion, which doesn't exist anymore. Because I was a new chief I just followed what the other Battalion Chiefs did. It was tradition. And the tradition was that you would pull up in front of the fire house and ring the bell. All gigs had bells on them. Because of economics, there are no more bells on gigs. This would be a signal for the men. If you're doing something you didn't want the chief to know about, you would stop doing it.

The man on the book would be there and everyone would line up alongside the apparatus. The chief would come in and inspect you. Make sure everybody was there; know what the roll calls were. Then go into the office with the captain; sign the book; discuss anything he had with the captain; take the material that was going out; and give the captain the material that was coming in. The man on the book would book everything by number. It was "General Order one eighty three, one eighty four, one eighty five." You would book each one individually. That it was brought in and it was accepted. He would book everything piece by piece that was going out. The captain would stay there. The journal was signed. The men had been dismissed previously after the chief inspected them and they would go about their business. You would leave. This was a tradition and it was a good tradition. Because you could keep track and know who was in work and who wasn't there. Who was supposed to be there and wasn't there and so forth.

Well, as a new chief I went to Engine Ten. I walked in. Nobody was there. I made it a habit not to go wandering around firehouses looking for trouble. So I sent the driver into the back to find out where everybody was. They came out and the fellow on the book asks, "Yes, can I help you chief?" I said to him, "You know, when I came here I thought you'd be on the book." and I explained to him the routine. He says, "We never do that for our chief. In fact he comes in the kitchen and sits down with us. He may have a beer. He may have a cup of coffee and he eats with us and then he leaves." I said, "Well, I don't operate that way. Where's the captain." He says, "The captain is upstairs in his room." You see the tradition was when the chief came in you hit the house gong. I said, "Well, get the captain down." He said, "Well, he worked all day and he's taking a nap." So, I hit the house gong at this point because I didn't want to go through a big explanation and the captain came down. I informed him that I was going to be there for two weeks and I didn't care how the other chief operated, but I want this policy to set forth. They did, but I'm sure when I left they went back to their old style.

Other houses were completely different. Now you take the same battalion on a different tour. You may go there to that same house and find that people followed a different procedure, either stricter, less strict, or somewhere in the middle. Leadership styles vary greatly.

Dunn: At the end of '64 I was promoted to captain and I was assigned to Engine Twelve on Belmont Avenue. The unique thing was that when I was assigned to Engine Twelve, I was the junior man in the firehouse. I had three senior firemen, firemen who had an extra five to ten years on my experience, all from the Central Ward. They were all on the job a long time. I felt very odd going in as a twenty-five year old captain to these people; knowing the experience they had in World War II. I believe Leo Broshuski worked himself up to be a captain in the Army from an enlisted man in World War II. Then for me to walk in as a young person and say, "Well, I'm the new captain of your firehouse now here's what I want."

George Fox, another World War II veteran, probably was one of the most knowledgeable people in the fire department at the time, particularly on apparatus and pumping. I had two regular firemen who were very good. We struck up a nice relationship. I followed their leads and slowly implemented changes as we went through the process. I also worked in conjunction with Truck Five, with Captain McCoy, who again was a very experienced captain. So, they really put me under their wings and made me a much better person.

I spent four years in Twelve Engine as a captain with that original crew the whole time. Nobody ever left and nobody ever came. The crew was always full. That's one of the differences I see today. Crews don't hold together as we did then. The changeover is much greater today. The vacancy rate is much greater today. So we actually built a team that worked very closely for almost five years together with no movement. I think it builds a much better fire company, when you can work that closely with the same guys. If you had a problem guy, I think he could have been corrected or the other three guys would have gotten him out of the house.

When I was promoted to Battalion Chief, I was assigned to the Second Battalion in downtown Newark. That was an excellent reason to leave Twelve Engine. Otherwise I'd probably still be struggling around over there.

My life as far as the fire department changed when I was promoted to Battalion Chief because I went to a different area. As a captain and a fireman in the Central Ward, you get locked into the firehouse. You realize you don't go out into the community, except for a minimum amount of inspections that you have to do. But when I went downtown it changed because now you went into visiting people. You went into Prudential. You would go over to a store like Bamberger's and talk about things and just pick up a lot of outdoor type of things. It also comes with being a Battalion Chief. You're out of the firehouse. I think the biggest change to becoming a chief officer is that you are not confined to the firehouse. You have your vehicle, at that time we had our aides. You want to become familiar with your district, so you're out on the road a lot.

The Second Battalion was quite a unique district because it was the high value district of the city of Newark, with major department stores like Bamberger's, Hayne's, and Ohrbach's. These buildings have two and three cellars in them and would have very complex problems if a fire occurred. This was a totally different type of firefighting than being in the ghetto, where you are going into basically three story frames. Each fire you responded to in downtown Newark was a different challenge. You were first due at a subway. You were first due at Penn Station which has the trains. A large part of the airport was the Second Battalion, also you had a large mercantile district, hardly any residential. Then on the far southern end of Frelinghuysen Avenue you rolled back into a heavily industrial area with a lot of chemical companies, paint companies, large industrial buildings. So I went from being a fire captain in a predominantly residential area to a Battalion Chief in a totally different area. But it also gave you a better, more rounded experience because you go into private fire protection.

I became very proficient in sprinkled buildings because everything is sprinkled in the downtown area. You're dealing with new technology in high rise buildings where there was computer programming. In your bank systems downtown on Broad Street, people were working twenty-four hours in a day which I was unfamiliar with until I was down there. I didn't understand that computers work at night. I thought they only ran eight to four o'clock and that's not true. When the bank shuts down the real people come and they have to input everything. So even though you have a high-rise fire at two o'clock in the morning, you could have fifty, sixty people on the top floor of a building doing this so you always have to be thinking.

That type of area was good for me because it did let you use all the knowledge you're reading in the books, such as the halon extinguishing systems, private alarm systems, water flow alarm systems, pre-active sprinklers. You would get calls from different stores when they were doing the new sprinklers asking which would be better. Bamberger's, which was the largest department store, had anti-freeze systems in their windows. Nobody is using that today because it slipped back into the water system and you can't do that. So I found it a much more challenging time because I applied a lot of the knowledge I had gained studying for captain. Now I could apply it to someplace. I was always impressed when I was in Bamberger's and I was doing a safety program with them. We were talking about replacing sprinkler heads. There are like 20,000 sprinkler heads in the building. The guy says, "We're going to start doing these. Where do you think we should start?" I'll never forget answering the guy "Well, I'd start in the basement." But in Bamberger's the basement is an open area; it's open to the public. I figured you start at the lower level and work up. The engineer looked at me and said, "Well, I'm going to start at the top because there are no people there." So, even though we're talking about a fire safety devise, the interest of the public fire person was life safety and interest of the company was very obvious. He was worried about his merchandise that he had stored on the upper floors. They did do it from the upper floors down.

But that's the difference of being the Battalion Chief in that type of an area. That was a rounded area. At the time I was promoted I really felt I wanted to stay in the Fourth Battalion, because that's where most of my experience and career was. When I reflect back on it now, it really rounded out my experience in the fire service by going downtown. It gave me a much wider experience. I learned how to deal much better with people. I realized that when you deal with executives that's a different perspective. If you want to talk to someone from the insurance industry or from the store security all you had to do was pick up the phone, say I'd like to see somebody, and you got a response. In the ghetto you just keep shoveling against the tide because you don't get a response from anybody about anything. That's the difference. When you did make a recommendation, people did listen to you. They did talk to you.

It's funny because, here it is a lot of years later and I had some new firemen. We brought them down to the subway a couple of weeks ago and gave them a tour of the subway. The subway in Newark is still non-sprinkled. It's still three stories down. It still moves a million people. There have only been two or three fires in it, which were mostly minor fires, but I went down and did my survey. I got a large packet in the mail the other day from the Department of Transportation. They're now looking to put a sprinkler system into this subway. They didn't know who to send the information to. So they sent it to me because mine was the only name they ever had.

So, it shows you that there are a lot of hazards in the city of Newark yet and they are being addressed more and more by government agencies. The Department of Transportation realizes that they have a problem there in the subway. There is no water down there. The chance of a major fire is very small but it is also very inaccessible to Newark Fire Department personnel. Sprinklers would be a big asset, particularly if they put pre-connected hose lines on the piping while they're doing it. It would save a lot of people a lot of work when there is an incident down there.

Carragher: When I got promoted to captain I went to Seven Engine. Chief Harold Davis was the chief in that house. It was an interesting thing, being in a house with Chief Davis. Harold lived down in Middletown and he used to like to take the three o'clock train on Friday. He would say, "Cap, why don't you hop the seat for a while?" Now here I am, I'm only a captain a month and he has me in the gig. That happened for a couple of weekends. Then one day he said to me, "You're going to be the Battalion Chief on Sunday. I took the day off, so you're acting Battalion Chief." Here I am now, a captain probably three months and I come in that morning about seven o'clock and I look up West Market to Morris. Here's a big four story apartment house all burned out and loads of companies all over it. I said,

"Oh my God." Now I have to go up as the acting Battalion Chief and say, "What am I going to do here? Look at the mess. All these companies, where do I start?" I'll never forget Bobby Dunbar. I walked up. Twenty Engine was working on the third or fourth floor and he said to me, "Cap, we'll stay here and do this. Why don't you get so and so to do this and so and so to do that?" I said, "That's sounds good." He gave me my first tip on how I should really start handling this thing and I did it. You appreciate things like this. I always remember Bobby doing that. That's how I learned. Going in there and give it a shot and you did.

Here I am at a four-alarm fire with maybe about fifteen companies there and no Deputy. The Deputy wasn't there because it was under control. The Deputy left. Then you have to start getting the overhauling done, but by around eleven o'clock or noontime we had everything under control. I had my first big one under my belt as an officer. That was an interesting fire. It wasn't the fire that was interesting. It was the newness. How you handled it. How you could do it. I'm sure it probably would have gotten done, but Dunbar was a big inspiration for me that day. He never realized it, but he was. I thanked him later on for that.

I fell into an excellent crew at Seven Engine when I went up there. Butterwhy was the captain in Seven Engine and he transferred to Three Truck. Somebody left Three Truck and went up to the Burg. I had one of the best crews you could probably want on the fire department. I had Ray McGee, Harry Uhde, Johnny Hughes, and Louie Formisano. You couldn't ask for a more respectful crew or a more aggressive crew. They were really a good crew all around. Harry Uhde, you'll probably never find another guy like him again, always thinking. Ray McGee always was thinking. Johnny Hughes was a young guy at the time, but Johnny Hughes was aggressive, wanted to do it. We jelled together. It was interesting there. I enjoyed Seven Engine.

I didn't stay that long. I stayed in Seven Engine I think probably less than a year. Again I'm always thinking, Six Engine has a vacancy coming up for a captain. I want Six Engine. It's busier, so I put a transfer request in through Harold Davis and asked for Six Engine. I went to Six Engine in 1966 and that's where I stayed.

When I went to Six Engine, I fell into another excellent crew. Wherever I went, it just seemed the crews were there. I had Henny Richter, Freddy Charpentier, Bill Costigan, and later Bobby Wiggins. You have to put personalities aside because if you take a crew like that, Charpy was one personality. Henny Richter was extremely opposite. Wiggins was another one and Costigan was another one. But together at a fire, you couldn't have anything better. They were excellent. They gelled and that's important as a crew. That was my crew from 1966 to 1970. We went to a lot of big fires up there.

Cody: I was promoted provisionally. I stayed in Four Engine on the first tour for a few months as a provisional captain. Then they transferred me to Two Truck on the third tour because they needed a captain over there. There was no captain and someone else wanted Four Engine on the first tour. So, I got bounced out there.

The provisional status bothered me more than it bothered anyone else. You were accepted as a captain because most of the guys didn't even understand it. As far as they knew you were promoted. They didn't give you much of a problem. My problem was I went to Two Truck after being on the job for six or seven years. I'm the captain and if you knew the guys I had; I had great guys. It was John O'Neill and Jerry Scanella. These guys were in their fifties then. I was like twenty-eight or twenty-nine years old and not ever working in the truck, I became the captain. I found it very difficult.

They made it easier for me. But you don't really want to work like that. If all your experience is in the engine, you want to go to an engine because you know your business. I got to learn the truck business.

The change from captain to Battalion Chief was kind of lonely. I mean, you had a crew and then you had no crew. When I was first promoted, I didn't get a spot. I was a roving chief and there were four roving chiefs. You just roved on one tour. They put you down at One Truck and you worked a particular tour. I was on the fourth tour, but you didn't do anything. You had no responsibilities. You had no gig. You just showed up and if someone was out sick or something, you would go to their spot.

You missed the guys you worked with. You missed your crew. I used to go back there all the time. I used to go back to Four Engine when I went to Six Engine. I used to go back and visit the crew, but that kind of diminishes, the need for that diminishes after a while, where you need to be with these people. After a while you realize that I'm growing. I'm moving on. And you don't need that as much.

I got my spot, about a year and a half after making Battalion Chief. I came to the Third Battalion in '84. So I was promoted in '83, July of '83. But the roving was good once all the other guys got spots. I was the last one to get a spot. So, I'm roving on all tours, but no one told me what to do. Where do I go? I can't come to the firehouse on every tour. Do I stay on the fourth tour? So, I called the Fire Chief's secretary, Joyce Rienhart. She said, "You go home and we'll call you." I like that.

There were no vacations. It wasn't the summer time. I believe it was January or something, so I went down to Florida. I came home and I heard nothing from them.

Then I get a letter in the mail and it's a schedule. Follow the schedule. I was scheduled through the year. I just worked that schedule. I would switch tours and I would work all the battalions, all tours. They always made time in between where I didn't overlap and if I did overlap then they would give me a time at the end. I had no one calling me. No agents looking for work. Like if there was a sick leave or something. Every now and then I'd get a call at home, "So and so in on sick leave. Come in and cover him." I'd say, "No, no. I just work by the schedule." Which was great, but that's the last time they've done that. After that the Battalion Chief had to come in. He had to come in in the morning and report in and cover any sick leaves. I never did that. So, I enjoyed that.

I got to see a lot of people. I worked every battalion on every tour and then I ended up over in the Third. Tony Maresca was retiring. Looked forward to going over there because when I came to the Third Battalion, this is where I got all my fires. So, I said this is a great spot. That was the end of the fires when I came here. We haven't had that many. I'm comparing with my times at Six Engine. Most guys in Six Engine always compare to Six Engine. Not everyone wants to hear that, but that's the way I always felt about it. I more or less got what I expected. I mean we had enough work. It's not like we didn't do anything.

The Battalion Chief's job is a different job all together. Where you had four or five guys to worry about now you have forty, forty-five guys to worry about and the details and the different things like that. Of course, there's always your mail run that you do every night. You're the fire department mail boy. But it was good. You spend so much time as a captain and then you're ready to move on to something else.

In terms of fighting a fire your duties change. Your duties as a firefighter change when you become a captain. As a firefighter you had done more or less what you were told. The captain called the shot and you did the work. As a captain if you were first on the scene, you called the shot for your company and did the work with them.

As a Battalion Chief you more or less call the shot for the whole fire, especially over in the Third Battalion. When I worked in the First Battalion or the Fourth Battalion, the Deputy was always right on your heels if not there before you. You got there and everything was kind of set up and then you were the inside chief. You more or less directed on the inside. But in the Third you have a little bit more time and you get to practice what you know and your tactics and strategies. You get to run the fire for a little while. At least until the Deputy comes and then you tell him what you did and how you set it up. Some Deputies will want to listen to what you did and some of them don't care what you did. They just come in and say, "Yes, yes, okay." Then you go in and you just do what you can wandering around. Wander around inside, see that the fire goes out. Hope that no one gets hurt.

Wargo: Well, I got promoted in 1978. I went from a slow truck company to a fairly busy One Engine. My first day that I was promoted I had that fire on Springfield Avenue and Williams Street, about four o'clock in the afternoon. It turned into a three alarm fire and it almost killed the third tour because there was a building collapse. Probably that is my most memorable fire because it is easy to remember the day. It was the first day I was on the job as a captain and that was one of the biggest fires I guess we had up to that time.

McGovern: It was a very big change going from firefighter to captain. Number one I was very young when I got made. I just turned twenty-seven years old when I got promoted, which is very young historically on the job. I went there as a new captain and I walked into a house where most of the guys had more than twenty years on the job. That right there is enough to make you a little nervous, but things worked out eventually. When you walk in the door it has to be, you either have to work with them or without them. If you can't work with me, the guys will leave and you fashion a crew. Eventually that's what happened. These guys were dynamite firemen. I loved the way they worked things. If you wanted something done, it was done. Maybe they didn't like the way I did things or I didn't like the way they did things. Eventually the guys who wanted to leave, left and new guys came in and they found their niche. But that's the way it went.

My biggest nightmare as a captain, what I always had it in the back of my mind, was losing a man. That was always in the back of my mind. I didn't care about myself. I just couldn't imagine going to somebody's wife. Telling them, Jesus Christ, he's dead. For the most part, I made it through my career, except for Mike DeLane. That was my nightmare as a captain, to lose a man. It was always in the back of my mind. That was the biggest transition because when you're a fireman you don't think of that. It's "What do you want?" I'll do it. And more so as a Battalion Chief, the odds go up. You don't have to worry about four guys, you have to worry about thirty.

There was a big-time change from captain to Battalion Chief. It's a whole other world. First you have thirty to thirty five guys' names. You walk in the door, you have to start remembering and every one of them has a different story. Everyone has a different want or need. When you're captain all you have to worry about is four little guys, your little world, very simple. Now the phone's ringing for silly stuff that you wouldn't believe.

Who needs this? Who needs that? Who's on sick leave? How am I going to fill this spot and at a fire you have to worry about thirty guys. Anybody who tells you they don't has to be whacked out. All it takes is one of your companies to screw up to make the rest of the ones coming in compound the screw up. By the time you get there, you have to straighten it out or see what's wrong. Why isn't this happening? Why isn't that happening? Are they safe doing what they're doing. It's a big difference. As a captain you're worrying about your three or four little guys. But then again I worry too much. That's the biggest change.

D. Prachar: I feel myself when I was promoted I was a little insecure about whether I could do it. There are a couple of men out there now who are captains, that if I was a fireman I would be afraid to work for. I really would. Some people who got promoted, put on a gray shirt, forgot where they came from. They were never firemen to begin with because you could always see them standing outside, full time pump operators, never an acting captain because they didn't want to go into the building and now they get promoted and are expected to be a leader.

There was bitterness, sour grapes. Going back to the time when we went all those years without an officer. Then to have an officer come in and you not like the officer who came in is beyond sour grapes. It's a hatred state. "You don't know what you're doing." Some of them don't.

Joe Ricca, when he got promoted they didn't like him because he was always drilling, constantly drilling as a captain, Battalion Chief, constantly drilling. I worked with Joe Ricca. When Joe was acting captain, we were out drilling. So he didn't do anything when he was a captain or when he was a Battalion Chief that he didn't do as a fireman. If he started all that after he got promoted, that was different. But he always did that and I'll always remember him for that. That he always did that. Even when the captain was there, the captain would say, "Well guys, he wants to go out and drill, take him out." And we did.

Now some of them are in positions, maybe in companies that they shouldn't be in, positions where they shouldn't be. Running a division or company, however you want to put it. They're not leaders. To me a leader is a man who is going to know when to go in, when to get out. Safety first. Not so much, "I am the captain" syndrome. "You go in and I'll wait here for you." There are some of them who just won't do that. Power, that's the word I'm looking for. "I have the power now. I can do this because I'm the boss." Shouldn't be there.

Some of the newer captains will rise up to the position if they come down off their high horse and realize what they have. If you have a company that's willing to work and you're not going to bust them so much. I don't mean you don't deserve to be on your high horse. As you get promoted everybody gets that little high. Same as when you come on the fire department. I got a high when I came on the fire department because I felt I was improving myself. As long as you improve and let the people around you improve also then it works. If you don't allow the people who are around you to improve somewhat with you instead of being on your high horse all the time, then you'll never improve. And I don't think you should go any further.

They should have taken into account how you work as a fireman and given some credit point wise, whether you deserve points to go for promotion. New York, a prime example, they have different classes of metals that you get for certain rescues and certain fires you do. You get points towards your test. One point could mean a lot of positions. It could mean a matter of one to twenty. Now if I'm going to be given one point because I had the knowledge out here in the field, that's going to help me. It'll help me as a fireman, as an officer, as I go on. But if I'm not getting that point out there, there's something wrong. I'm not doing my job.

When I got promoted I had that attitude that my shit don't stink. But then I had to come back down to earth and say, "Hey, last week I was one of them. This week I am one of them, only I changed uniforms." So, I learned to work hand in hand with the guys. Although becoming the boss, letting them know that I was the boss, but we still work together. I had that with the companies I was in. Seven Engine, young crew raring to go, but I had to slow them down, to look before you go in the building. The old school was you always look before you went in for your second way out. Seven Engine just charged right in. Not even look. All they see is fire. I didn't slow them up to the point where I said you're not going into the building, but on the way in let's walk and let's look at where we're heading. Let's look for a way out if we get in a jam, which worked out with that crew.

Going to where I'm going now, I have a couple of senior men. One of them likes to run the company, so I'm going to butt heads with him. But I have no problem with that because I'm not a drinker. The guy likes to have his beer. I never believed in drinking in the firehouse. I didn't when I came on the job, while I was a fireman. As an officer I still don't believe in it. Coming from Belmont Avenue back when that was the boozers, whatever, I've been challenged since I've been a captain. One time, with the statement, "You? Coming from Belmont Avenue, the biggest lushes on the job." I said, "Prove it. Prove that I was the lush. Prove that I drank in the firehouse. There isn't a man on this job who can say they saw me drink a can of beer in the firehouse." That's proving my point.

Had a man in Rescue on the first tour challenge me. I called Five Truck on the first tour and had this man talk to the guys there. He was told no matter what they had on the table, when I walked in the door, they always brought out a bottle of Pepsi because that's what I drank. If I was to have that problem now, I would think nothing of giving the men a warning that I don't appreciate it. I don't condone it. I won't condone it. The second time I will have the man write. The third time, it will probably be hard, but I really think I would put the man on charges because it's my life.

I've seen guys die on this job, firemen who I know might have been drinking, had a couple of beers. I don't think that I'll allow it and have a family come back to me and say, "Do you know this man was drinking?" That might have been the cause of why he died. For the life of me, I would not be able to take that, so therefore I will not allow it in my house. Although when I was younger, when I was off, I did my share. God knows I did my share. But in the firehouse, I've come in a couple of times with hangovers. Sorry I came in, but in those days you came in. Nowadays you don't come in because you're sick. But I came in and I was lucky enough to have an officer who I could work things out with. Like I said, guys came in, go to bed. This is one of the few times where they would let you, but that's attitudes. It goes back to attitudes. Everything comes back again. What goes around comes around.

Finucan: When you reach Deputy Chief, the closeness of the fire department is lost. People at my level don't really know what people are thinking any more. You're just not that close to them. They yes me to death. They could be doing that because of the eagles. They could "Yes, sir." Everything that I say could be "Yes, good idea. Fine, we like it that way." I have no way of telling what's going on out there anymore.

It's not like you're in an engine company. When you're in an engine company and you're a captain, a company officer, you're just a step above a firefighter and you're part of that big family out there. You really more or less know what's going on because there are more captains out there who will tell me I'm a complete asshole because I'm the same rank as they are. But as you move up the ladder there are fewer and fewer people who can actually give you that feedback. I mean there's only ten or twelve other Deputy Chiefs who can say anything like that to me. And they just don't. They're not that type of guy. So, you lose it as you move up. You lose that feeling of what's really going on out there.

McDonnell: For me there was an adjustment from firefighter to captain. I can't say for anybody else, but for me, I didn't even want it. I tried to turn it down. It was a real big adjustment for me. When I was a fireman I just ran around, did whatever I wanted to do and then all of the sudden now you're responsible not only for yourself, but for four or five other people.

When I studied I don't think that was something I ever thought about. I never really thought about what I was getting myself into. I just more or less thought about taking the test and doing well on the test. It was the competition to do well on the test that made me study as much as I did. I never really thought about what I was getting myself into. So, it was a major adjustment for me. It was hard. If it hadn't been for the building collapse with Ray, I would have never stayed.

I had already tried. I had gone down and told them I didn't want the job. I had talked with my brother. He just said, "Try it, try it." So I promised him I'd give it a shot for a while. Then my first day is when we had the building collapsed. After that I felt I couldn't. I'd look like a coward, that I didn't want the responsibility. Now I actually didn't want the job. After that I couldn't, couldn't quit. I was stuck now. But for me it was a major, major adjustment, something that is not really emphasized to guys.

Your whole perspective changes. As a fireman I could be as reckless as I wanted. It was my life. I could go do things. I did things that I would kill somebody if they did them when they were working for me. I don't know how the captains ever put up with the stunts I pulled. I don't know. Going into a burning building by myself, nobody else in there. Steal somebody's line and go put the fire out with the place falling. "Where were you?" "I was in the alley."

It was a much bigger responsibility. You have to give orders where somebody else's life is in danger. Plus, it's a big change, too. Now you have to make sure that things are done. You have to make sure other people do their job. Where before you just did what you had to do. You didn't really have to worry about what the next guy was going. If he wasn't doing his job, it wasn't your responsibility.

All of the sudden you become a captain. You have to be concerned about guys coming to work, getting there on time. Doing what they're supposed to do, doing their chores around the firehouse, doing their training. It was a big, big change. It changed the job completely. I always said if I had it all to do over again, I never, never would have been a captain. The most fun I ever had was as a fireman. I guess I'm not the kind of person who cares about authority or position or anything like that. It took a lot of the fun out of the job for me. That responsibility, I took that responsibility seriously. It was a big, big change. I think that's something they should emphasize to people, before they become captains. Talk to guys when they're firemen and say there's a big, big difference. It's not just a pay raise. That's what, unfortunately, a lot of people just think of. Oh, I'm going to make more money. But there's a lot more that goes along with it.

T. Grehl: When I got promoted, I went to Twenty-seven Engine for one month. Chief Bob White called me in his office and says to me, "Why are you here? What are your intentions?" I said, "Well, I don't want to marry your daughter." He wanted my intentions. "I'm out of here as soon as I can get out of here." He says, "Okay, because then I have to find somebody." So, I was there for one month. I got promoted the end of November of '77 and January first I went to One Engine.

It was a change because I went from the truck to an engine, but you know what, I used to take a lot of details. We didn't get that many, but when we did get some details I would take them. I'm a young guy. A lot of the old timers would say, "Ah, a detail. I don't want to go on detail." Especially if they were to Five Truck or a company uptown, I would take it. I'm young. I want to learn. I want to learn what's going on. So, I went to One Engine.

I worked with a good crew and I learned from them. We learned as we went along. Caught a lot of fires. Caught a lot of second alarm fires because One Engine caught every second alarm in the city. Then South Broad Street started burning Chestnut Street, Orchard Street, and South Broad down by South Street. So, we caught a lot of first due fires. It was good. I totally enjoyed it. I wanted to get busy and I wanted to go with the best at the time which I thought was Six Engine. Then my hand was forced because they closed One Engine. So, my wish came true in a roundabout way.

I walked in the first day at One Engine. We had the fire on South Orange and Springfield, Music City. We relieved at that fire. We came on that night. It was going good. The first tour had it. They took the hydrant. They were right in front of the building. I don't know how that happened, but they had a hydrant right in front of the building. Well, I had to write all night because the building collapsed on One Engine. My first night as a captain at One Engine I had to write why the building collapsed on us. We lost the bell, which we don't have anymore. We lost the bell, the siren, the bumper..

It was a transition from fireman to captain. I'm not big into power, whatever you want to call it. I try to be the same because I saw some people go from fireman to captain and become different people. I swore if that was ever me, I always wanted to try to maintain the same person I am. Obviously, you have a certain amount of discipline. There are a certain amount of things you have to do. Maybe I was wrong, but I always tried to be friends with the people I worked with, understand them. Not like a big father, big brother, but I figure if everybody is happy, we work together happy. I didn't have a big problem with that because I always worked with good people.

I really didn't care about the power. I didn't care about the prestige. I didn't care if they called me captain. It didn't matter. I didn't have to wear a uniform. A lot of people, when they get promoted, "I want my bars. See my bars." I didn't care. I mean I would walk around in a fireman's shirt. It didn't matter to me. I liked the job better. Obviously, it was better. Being the boss is always nicer, but as far as all the other stuff, I don't think I had a problem with it. Only once or twice did you have to use the discipline that is inherent with the job, maybe in One Engine and maybe twice in Six Engine. It's the easiest job in the world if you just let it happen. If you have good guys, they make it easy. They make it real easy.

I had guys who just went and my concept of an engine captain was always to be immediately behind the tip man. That was my concept. I don't know if it was right. He had the tip because that's the fireman's job and my job is to be right with him, on his coat, no matter where he goes, I'm going. I had bulls. As far as giving orders at fires, I just went where the guys went. It was like, what do you think? Okay, let's do it. I worked with those bulls. They just dragged me along. I just happened to go with them. I think you find when you get with some companies that you have to say, "Okay, let's pull the ceiling here. Let's get the line in this room." I always worked with people who would say, "You want to get out of the way, Cap? We're going to pull over here. I'm going to get this." That makes it easy. That makes the transition easy. As opposed to saying we have to do this, we have to do that.

Ryan: I made captain in 1989. Was captain of Eleven Engine on the third tour. Moved to the new firehouse, was there for about eight, nine months and Eleven Engine on the third tour was put out of service. Transferred from there to Ten Engine on the third tour. Was captain at Ten Engine on the third tour. Went to Engine Twenty-one for a short period of time and was made chief in 1996 in the Ironbound section. Since being chief, it's been interesting because it's a different thing than the actual application of stream or aerials. I had some great haz-mat incidents and coming down here has been different because you have to apply all of the things you studied over the years.

It's been a great experience for me being chief, actually being able to implement the different strategies and tactics. Haz-mat, some major fires, I've had some really good major fires and worked them out pretty well by using the stuff in the book. It's a constant growing process. I don't know where they're going in the future. The people who had the experience from the years of a lot of fires are rapidly dwindling from the job. The young fellows who are coming up, to their detriment and blessing to them too, they didn't get pounded with it. But they didn't get the experience. So, if they're not students, I don't know where they're going to learn it from.

H. Carter: Park Avenue when I went there was a real hold over from the old days. I had an older crew. My Battalion Chief in the First Battalion when I was in Eleven was Richie Hettinger. A man who I greatly admire, who's lessons I carry with me and will use if they ever release me from Training to be a real Battalion Chief in the field. We had a promotion party and as with all things in Eleven Engine, the tradition was, "You want a party? You buy the party yourself." Everybody had a birthday party, but everybody paid for their own birthday party, same with promotions. So, I had my favorite meatloaf and mashed potatoes and Chief Hettinger bought a bottle of Barbarone Red, Battalion One had a gallon of it. Rocco Piegaro his driver bought a six pack of diet seven-up to cut it because he knew I didn't like sugar in my soda.

We're having the festivities. Chief Grehl was there. I was there. We're all drinking wine. Hettinger stands up and says, "I want you folks to know that I'm counting on Harry when he goes to Park Avenue to straighten things out. I want him to teach those people what the white stuff is on the back of the fire truck." Meaning the hose. Because at the time Fifteen had a terrible habit of rolling up the street, stopping at the corner of Sixth Avenue just out of sight so Eleven would come blazing in. We'd have to drop the three inch, the two and a half and put all the water on the fires in that area.

The first month I'm on Park Avenue, we get a box for Sixth Avenue and North Thirteenth Street. I can see the smoke on the horizon. So, we pull up to the corner, I lean out of the cab, and I raise my hand and I yell "Two. Drop two." You thought I stuck a knife in the heart of the two guys on the back step. We dropped a wet three inch and a dry two and a half. This is when we only had the three inch and two and a half inch lines. And laid the whole bed both sides down the block. I guess it was about eleven months later that all those guys transferred out. This would have been in the middle of '78 when they had the big hire. Hired a ton of guys between May and September.

Jack Glass, the captain on Seven Truck, and I had been down to see the Director. We were trying to dump our crews because we had some older, less productive people, nice guys in most cases. Comes the revolution in January of '79, there was a lot of roving going on trying to balance roll calls through the summer of '78 and into the fall of '78. In January of '79 they assigned new crews to Park Avenue. Three guys and Elton Fisher with Jack, Elton was the hold over. I had Jay Corbo staying as my driver and three new guys on the back. As I recall it was Phil Daly, Andy Truskowski, and Jim Titcomb.

Jack and I really did drill in those days. That was before the general malaise set in and we stopped doing anything. It couldn't have been a better time. We had all the guys certified to drive, Phil on the pumper and the truck, within thirty days. And then the winter that year, the winter was the busiest winter I can ever remember. Between like the end of January and the middle of April, we went to a working fire, minimum every shift day and night. We really did learn how to fight fire that winter.

Langenbach: Big mistake. No, not a big mistake getting promoted. That was just like an evolution, I went from Twelve Engine fireman to Twelve Engine captain. I realized it too late. Should have never done that. Same guys. Big mistake. Especially because when I got promoted, then I got demoted and I stayed in the same house. I always advised people after that. If you get promoted, don't stay in the same house. You should go somewhere else. It's very comfortable to do that, but it's also difficult at the same time because there's a whole different perspective when you're a captain.

So, when I got the chance, when Schimpf got promoted. Schimpf went to Six when Jimmy Cody got promoted and that's how I got the spot in Twelve because I roved. When I first got promoted, I roved. Horrible. And then I went to Twelve and then when Schimpf got promoted, I went to Six. I jumped on it right away. For that reason, because these are my friends and I couldn't be their boss.

I knew everybody up at Six, Bird and George and Artie, but it was different, a whole different relationship than these guys who I lived with for years. But yes it's a big difference. When you're a fireman, especially during my time as a fireman, we always had captains who looked out for us. The captain made sure you didn't go completely nuts and do something stupid. So, now that's your responsibility as a captain, to make sure your firemen don't go completely nuts. I'm working with guys who are very, very aggressive. Now I'm being cautious. I don't want to get anybody hurt. You know, "Eh, nothing's going to happen to anybody here while I'm working." A guy gets burned I take it home and I'm sick. But yes, it's a whole different world. Interesting dynamic when you become a boss. And as you go up further it's even worse.

At the time I moved up to captain at Twelve, it seemed like this was a great thing. This was going to be a perfect fit because now I'm just going to be Jim, the captain. Except the first thing the fire department does is they isolate you. You're the captain. Now you have your own little room. No more in the bunkroom, now you have your own little room up there. You have all this responsibility. I never had this before. Acting captain, who cared? You wrote the book. You didn't write the book. Whatever. Now they expect you to do all that stuff. Paperwork has to go in. Plus you are also responsible for what happens, the outcome of everything. You're used to hanging on the back step of Twelve Engine and the captain's calling the shots. Now you're sitting up front and you have to say, "We're going to do this. We're going to do that. We're going to go here. We're going to go there." It's a very, very different.

Before I got promoted to Battalion Chief, I went down to the Academy because Andy Wargo was getting ready to retire. They asked me if I wanted to come down because I had been down there a couple of times on light duty. So, I came down to the Academy. I had taken all the classes before. I had all my certificates, so I came down and worked with Andy for a while. Then Andy retired and I stayed on. I got promoted out of the Academy. Then I went roving a little bit and then went back to the Academy. Stayed there, then I went to the Arson.

I roved for just a month or two, it wasn't very long. In fact I was at the Academy and I'd bounce out of there and go out and fill in a vacation trick or something like that. Go back out and fill out another vacation trick then go back unless somebody's off or something like that.

I ended up in Arson after I got a call from Bobby Fitzpatrick. They were just in the middle of investigating an entrance list. I guess it wasn't working well because there was no boss up in Arson. It was all captains. I was a Battalion Chief then. So they said, "Would you go up to Arson?" So, I went up there and took over the Arson Squad. I thought I was just there to get the investigations rolling because that's all I did. I spent the whole first three months up there doing nothing but candidate investigations. But then I moved over and went into the arson part of it.

Perdon: I got promoted in June of '95. I had no problem with the transition. It was just another day. I did some roving, which probably helped out. Made everything go nice and easy. Then I went to Eighteen Engine. So, I had a good crew. I had Flanagan. They were good. Them boys can put out some fire. And then from there I went back to Six. Then from Six I got bounced around. That's okay though. Spent some time at Fourteen. Then I went to Ten Engine, good crew there. Then to Twenty-eight Engine. I went from like not moving for twenty years to traveling all over the city.

Ricca: Making captain was a change for the better. After fifteen years as a fireman things starting to get a little bit dull. It was like a new job, like a new life. It was starting all over, like a kid going to school. I remember the first day with the uniform on, the helmet, getting used to being Cap. Getting used to not picking up, but asking somebody, "Let's get this and do that or do this." At a fire, not "Hey get the roof, ventilate." Finally being the guy who would tell somebody else what to do.

I went to Twelve Engine. Finucan had been gone a while though. The crew had worked for a long time without a captain and they were used to their way. It was not that I came in with a tyrant's way of doing things, it was just a little bit more uniformity. Because Boisey did stuff that Boisey knew was right. The lines in the book, the time in the index, Boisey would take the journal and draw the line and time and index each line until he did the whole book. Nobody does that anymore.

They'd make up the watch schedule. I told them, "You decide who's driving. I don't want to decide it, but somebody's got to drive and the truck has to be ready." So, they had their own little schedules down. They had it down to where it worked out. We never got caught with, "It's your turn, your turn, your turn." The bell rang. I knew who was on the book. They had their own little ways, but it was for the good. They all did the right thing. Charlie Crenshaw complained and complained, but the guy's a hell of a fireman, hell of a fireman.

During my first night we lost a baby on Hillside Avenue. This house was going stem to stern. First due and now Twelve Engine really, its first due area is down to nil. And we get a first due fire. I had two first due fires, I think, my first night. Lady yelling, "My baby's in there." And it was a white lady and something just didn't click right. She was in the house next door. Why is your baby in here? So me, Charlie Crenshaw and Boisey, we go plunging in. I'm saying, "Come on guys, we've got to push. We've got a kid here." Five Truck's right behind us. Going through, going through, knock the fire down. Now we're searching. Poor little thing looked like a ham, that's how badly it was burned. Felt like shit because we lost a kid.

Once again always doing that act; "What if we did this or that?" And I turned to Tommy McDonnell and I told him, I said, "I never thought it was this hard to be a captain." I said, "Now I know what you felt like." I used to see the pain on Tommy's face when we got hurt and that's what it came down to. Like he said, you don't realize it. I thought it was, you just sit up there, ring the bell and then supervise, but not knowing that when your guy gets hurt, you get hurt. That's why I used to see the pain on Tommy's face with Ray, all of us when we got hurt. It's like having kids.

I've got Boisey, Calvin Jackson, and Charlie was there. But I had a company where I didn't have to say anything to them. The only problem I found with them at the beginning was I like to bring my own water supply in. They coined the phrase "Captain stretch a lot." Because we got a couple of times where companies used to go in and come behind you without water because they wanted a piece of it too. I learned. I said, "We're bringing our own water in." Especially with Chief Smith, Chief Smith demanded. If guys didn't bring water in and he thought they skated, after the job, he'd make them stretch back to the hydrant and that's how it should be.

Now, guys open the hydrant, it's dead, "I'm done. We can go home." I've always been blessed to have a good crew. New guys, you like to have new guys because you train them the way you want them to be trained. The right way, the wrong way, and your way I guess is what it comes down to. But I always had good guys, thank God. I've kissed the ground for the crew I have. They don't let me touch a thing. I feel the captain's job isn't to have the tip. If the captain has the tip, there's something wrong with the company. My job is to make sure they're safe. They're job is to put the fire out with me making sure they're safe.

We've had little problems every now and then but that's what happens when you get a bunch of guys together. Sometimes we're our own worst enemies. We complain about watching TV. You've got a hundred and fifty-two channels and nobody can find a show to watch. But other than that I've always been lucky. That's why I stayed on Belmont Avenue.

Gesualdo: You could say there was a cultural shock or a resentment syndrome when I got promoted, but thank God when I walked in to Ten Truck, it was a great bunch of guys, all mature guys. I actually called up from the Training Academy. I heard I was going to be sent to Ten Truck prior to coming out of the captain's school down there. I called up and asked the guys if they had a problem with that and if they think it would be an issue, I would find somewhere else. I said, but the spot's open. I would like to come back there.

I didn't seem to have any problems with any of them. It was all service guys. Bob Bowie, Charlie Krutulis, Don Janus all the guys had been in the service, went through probably the same situation while they were in the service. Seeing guys promoted. So, I really can't say there was a big problem for me. If anything it was probably a benefit as a truck captain, having only sparsely worked as a truckman for a while and learning everything I could from guys like Charlie Krutulis and Bob Bowie and Don Janus. They knew just about all there was to know about truck work and I only knew about half of what was involved. But I got well-schooled by being sent to Truck Ten. I learned a lot of truck work from those three individuals.

The transition was harder for me I think than it was for them. It was harder for me to go from the engine to the truck. Not putting either company down, but I always found engine work to be a little more initially aggressive, initially exciting. Truck work seemed to be a little scaled back kind of approach to me. It just didn't seem to have the same excitement as working on an engine. But then some guys probably feel the same way about the truck. Maybe it's just the way I looked at it. Maybe it's twelve years on an engine and I was spoiled, but I definitely found myself being more energized being on an engine.

I wasn't worried about feeling responsible for the men. I was worried about them feeling responsible for me because they knew a whole a lot more than I did. They said, "We have to train this son of a bitch real fast." But it came. It came real easy. And like I said, they were very patient and understanding and there wasn't any resentment at all.

I guess you always remember your first one when you're in a command position. Now instead of just yourself to worry about, you have four other people, sometimes more. I can remember a fire right down the street on

Bergen where it was two buildings involved, slate roofs. So there was a lot of ladder work, roof ladders involved. I remember being hollered at by one of my men because I was doing too much physical labor and not enough commanding. I thought to myself, "I don't have to tell you guys what to do. Chris, you've been truckmen for ten, twelve, fourteen years." But that was they're way of saying to me, step back and do what you're supposed to do and don't feel like you have to do all the physical labor. I think a lot of officers are probably guilty of that in their first few months or few fires. They want to revert back to their firefighter days. That's probably your biggest stepping stone, your biggest hurdle as an officer, to realize that you have to stand back now, observe, make decisions, and put people in situations. You can't do that if you're raising ladders and stretching hose. So that was an eye opener, my first job on Bergen and Shephard.

Chapter Six: Firehouse Humor

F. Grehl: When I was a Battalion Chief and roving, I was in the Third Battalion and someone called me up. McLaughlin was the Deputy Chief then. He was a former truckman and loved to go out and take inventories of the equipment on the truck and things like that. "Where's you six footer?" Surprise things, he would jump in the firehouse. I never surprised. I would always tell them. "I'm coming. We're going to drill or something like that."   Anyway, they tell me McLaughlin is out and he's getting every company that he going into. He's telling them, "Take the apparatus out and put up a church raise." Well, that's a tough one if you don't do it. You've got to train.

I get a tip that he's going to sneak up to Six Truck. Well, Six Truck doesn't know from nothing, very little practice or anything else. So, I real quick run up to Six Truck and I get the captain. I said, "Run upstairs and get your Oklahoma ladder book down." He did. I get everybody. "This is what we're going to do." We went through the process. Then I ran. I left. Lo and behold, McLaughlin shows up. Says to them, "Get the apparatus out. Okay, Cap. See how good you are. Put up a church raise." Well, the thing went up beautiful, the ropes and all. He says, "That God damn Grehl was here wasn't he?"

He got even with me. I was in the Second Battalion and I went for a ride on the fireboat. Never been on the fireboat, so as a Battalion Chief the guys said, "Would you like to go for a ride?" We went out on the river, riding around, come back, and the gig is gone. I can't find the gig, the driver either. Where did it go? Nobody knows. So, I call up One Engine to see if he's over there because that's where he rode out of. Not there. Two Engine was still up the street. No, can't find them. I said, "I don't know where the hell he is."

So, I got a ride back to One Engine. I go back there and McLaughlin looks at me. He says, "What are you doing here?" I said, "Someone stole the gig. I have to come back and write a report." He says, "What do you mean someone stole the gig?" I said, "They also kidnapped the driver. I have a big report to write." I go upstairs and I get the papers out. He comes upstairs. "Are you really going to write that report?" I said, "Certainly, I can't find him anywhere. Try to get him on the radio, he doesn't even answer." He said, "Well, Sonny, I went down there and I asked the driver 'Where's the Chief at?' He said, 'He's out riding in the fireboat.' 'He is huh? Well, let's see what he does when he comes back and there's no gig. Take the gig, go down to Nineteen, and put the captain in as acting Battalion Chief.'" That's what he did to me.

Another funny story. We had an old, old Ward LaFrance as a spare. The thing wouldn't go up Springfield Avenue faster than the buses. We were at the end of the year and were talking about how we need another run to beat Twenty Engine. Havic is driving. He pulled the apparatus in front of the apron and is backing in when the apparatus catches fire. The captain is hollering, "Put the pumps in. We'll put it out. We'll put it out." Havic's hollering, "No, call Twenty Engine. Give them another run." "No, we can't give Twenty Engine a run." They're out in the middle of the street and the engine's on fire.

Another time we had one of those old American LaFrances and we were at the fire. I think it was Twenty Engine was ordered to take up. They were a little bit in front of us and so they're backing out of the street. They catch our bumper, the front bumper. It just pulled the bumper from where it holds onto the frame. There are two connections on the frame. Just pulls it out, straight and they take off. The captain comes back and asks, "Bernie what happened to the fire engine." He says, "I don't know." "What do you mean you don't know? You're supposed to be standing here. You're the driver." Well, how are we going to explain this? Nobody wants to write these eleven page accident reports. We go back to the firehouse in the middle of the night, three, four o'clock in the morning. That center post between the two bays, we put big blankets and cushions on the concrete and Bernie Havic goes running into the wall with the bumper, pushing it back. Well, we pushed it all back, but of course the captain got a call about drunken firemen. They were running into the firehouse, can't get it in the door. So we got around that.

I was down the Academy one day teaching a class and Andy Marcell was in the class. They have a big meeting in Eddie Wall's office about the leaky Nomex coats. There was a break and Andy asked, "What are they doing there?" "They're having a meeting about what they're going to do about these coats. They're leaking so badly." "Oh." Next thing you know Andy goes out to the apparatus and comes back in. He's got his Nomex coat on, his helmet, and his boots. He goes over and knocks on Chief Wall's door, "Come in." He opened the door and Chief Wall said. "Yes, Andy, what can I do for you?" Andy says, "Well, you're having a meeting about what we can do to prevent these Nomex coats from leaking." The Chief says, "Yes." Andy says, "I have an idea." "Oh, what's your idea?" He's standing there with all his gear on. Behind him he has an umbrella. He opens an umbrella. Naturally, they threw him out. There were chiefs from all over the state and manufacturers and everything else. Andy Marcell pulls that.

Masterson: If you have thin skin, go get another job. The firehouse was great. The guys worked together. We were always busting and carrying on. I mean there was no social tea. Don't make a mistake because they'll let you know it. And the less amount of work you got, the worse it got. You needed work to keep everybody moving and happy. As long as you had work you were fine.

They did a lot of silly things. I don't know if they're jokes. I mean they weren't jokes. They were always carrying on with something. Gordon Henry was in Five Truck. He was a piece of work. The first tour had him on a chair. They put two hooks under the legs of the chair and they had him up on their shoulders. He's sitting up in the chair with a brown paper bag on his head. He took an old sheet and put it around him. They go walking up Belmont Avenue and he's blessing all the derelicts.

The city was working in Five Truck and the masons were there. They were out there working on something and all the cinderblocks and sand and cement were all out in the yard. So, I go to bed and those guys are sitting around restless, nothing to do. So what do they do? They go out and they mix up a load of cement in the box and they cement up Twelve Engine's door. They were blocked in. I went out in the morning. I looked. I said, "Oh, my God." I just kept going. I got in my car and drove away. Like I said, if you're thin skinned, get another job. That's the way it was in the firehouse. Five Truck, oh, it was brutal. Especially if they saw they got under your skin. You're dead now. You're dead. They'll never let up.

Freda: The ball-busting syndrome that probably exists in a firehouse like it does in no other profession. They completely break each other's balls. I call it testicular waggery. It went on constantly.

A. Marcell: We had an awful lot of fun. My God, I enjoyed going to work. I worked with guys who laughed so hard one guy had to go to the hospital. We were in the firehouse one day with two young kids just on the job. I said, "What can we do with them?" We took peanut butter, wiped it on the side of my shoe and one of the guys came in and said, "Hey, Marcell, you stepped in dog shit." I said, "I did not." He says, "Yes, look at your shoe." I said, "Oh, wait a minute." I sat down and put my finger in it and put my finger in my mouth. I said, "You're right. That is dog shit." The two kids' eyes got big. Then about a week later, we were at a fire and the guy said, "Hey, there's that guy who eats dog shit."

One time Patty DiGioccimo walked in about a quarter after five in the winter. It was just starting to get dark. He said, "Look what I have, Marcell." He took a box out and opened it. There was a gorilla outfit inside. My God, that thing looked real. I said, "Here comes one of the guys. Go upstairs and put the thing on." He went put the suit on upstairs. This guy walked in. I said, "Hey, some gorilla just escaped from a zoo in New York." He said, "Yes?" I said, "What would you do if you saw a gorilla and it grabbed you." "Well, you have to show that you're not afraid of them. They can smell that you're scared." I said, "Jesus Christ, I would be afraid." He started to go upstairs and I said, "Hey, wait a minute. He was just seen on top of a truck coming up Central Avenue." He ran down. "Wait," I says, "There's a bulletin. There's going to be more news about it." He says, "Well, I'm going upstairs to change. If you hear it, call me and I'll come down." So he walked up the stairs.

Patty stood behind a locker and as this guy walked in, he went "Uhrah" and grabbed him. I never heard such a merciful scream in my life. He ran across the floor, slid down the pole, and he couldn't get off the floor because his leg was twisted under him. This guy came down the stairs with the suit on.

To make a long story short, they put me on charges. I went down to see Chief Redden and he told me, "Marcell, are you crazy? You could have killed this guy. You know that don't you?" And I said, "Well, we were only fooling around." He said, "Explain to me what happened." I explained to him. He said, "Did you pull a down watch last night?" I said, "Yes." He said, "Well, that's your punishment. I'd give anything in the world to see that."

Another time I was driving a chief. We were responding down Frelinghuysen Avenue. We got almost past Nineteen Engine when the captain called a three oh five. So, we turned around and we're coming back. The chief's fit to sleep. He put his head against the window and he's asleep. So I call the operator and said, "Battalion Five is available." Then I stopped. There was a tractor-trailer truck backed into a loading dock. All that was there was the big front of it. You know, the big radiator grill and all that. I pull right up next to it and put the overhead light on. He's now sleeping. I put the siren on. It was going "woowoo." I shout, "Watch it!" He woke up, looked, and saw the front of the truck. It looked like the truck was slashing into us. And he went "ooooow". We went back to the firehouse. He said he was going to put me on charges. He said he's deathly sick and he had to go home. He told Chief Griggs that. Chief Griggs said, "You phony bastard." He went "rah-rah" like he was throwing up and had to put Formisano in the gig.

A mechanic from Mack Trucks came in once. We had a brand new Mack engine that had a lot of little flaws on it. They had to fix them. This mechanic said, "You guys don't know how to drive the Mack. You don't know what you're doing." Then he said "I'm going to check the brakes." I said, "Be careful. The brakes don't work on this." He said, "You don't know how to work them." He got on the creeper and he slid underneath the engine.

We had a tire in the back where you keep all the coats. We rolled the tire out. Shook the rig and said, "Watch it! This is rolling. I know it is." He said, "Shut up." Then we rolled the tire over his legs. He let out a merciful scream. He came out pure white. He thought the God damned rig went over his legs. He called Kossup on the telephone. Two minutes later Kossup called back and said, "Detail Marcell out of the firehouse." Anytime he'd come to fix the rig he wouldn't do it unless I was detailed out. They'd detail me to Seven Engine.

Miller: I'll never forget. This one guy, he was late for work. His was supposed to come in at six o'clock. He says, "Cap, I'll be late coming in." The captain says, "Okay, take your time." Then the captain says, "Where is he?" at ten o'clock. Still wasn't there. He calls up again, he says, "I'm still coming in, Cap." The captain says, "Okay." We were one and three. "You'll be in. Don't worry about it." Still didn't come in. One o'clock in the morning, two o'clock in the morning, four o'clock, five o'clock in the morning he calls up. And he says, "Cap, I'm still on my way in." Then the captain asks him, "Well, where are you?" He says, "Right now I'm in North Carolina." He was driving in from Florida. He was going to be a little late. He didn't get in until the next day.

Cody: The pole on High Street was in a closet. It was recessed into the wall. It was a normal pole hole on top, but when you slid down you came into a closet. We used to have fun with that where they used to put a two by four through the doors on the bottom, hit the gong and the guys would pile up in the pole hole and the other guys would pour water in. Childish, but fun at the time. It was fun at the time.

Garrity: Well, we decided that since Skylab was going to fall out of the sky that we should go up on the roof and watch it. We decided that we should take our beach chairs and all our accruements, get up on the roof and have a good time. Started out fine and it degenerated into a bottle throwing contest. We actually went out and painted a target on Avon Avenue. It started with a garbage can in the ally. We're dropping the bottles down into the alley. That was no fun. So we decided to throw them over the roof into the garbage can. That was fine for a while. Somebody broke a bottle on the front of the fire house, one of the civilians. So we decided it was only fair that we retaliate and with that like nine bottles went off the roof. And then it started into a bottle throwing contest. It lasted about an hour. The Battalion Chief came up and started giving us a lot of shit, so we were going to stuff him down the scuttle hole and drop him if he didn't leave us alone.

The next night when we came to work, someone put a Kotex with ketchup on it in his room. So, he's upstairs and he comes down in a huff. He wants a line up. He hits the house gong and everybody comes out and we line up. He says, "Which one of you guys thinks I'm a woman?" And with that the whole two crews took one step forward. And he's starting up. I said, "Don't give me any shit." "You can't do this to me. I only want a little respect." I said, "That's all you're going to get is a little respect. If you mess with us, we're going to mess back." Comes dinnertime now, instead of being twelve places set, there's only eleven. Everybody sitting but him. "Where am I sitting?" "You're not eating here anymore. If you're going to fool with us, you can go someplace else to eat." It took him about three weeks and he apologized. He was going to put us all on charges. He was going to do this. He was going to do that.

McGovern: I have a practical joke that nobody ever knew about. Chief McCormack at the time was Deputy Three and he was in the house with us in Rescue. He had this white dress cap that he wore all the time, but it was filthy. I mean it was filthy from all the smoke because he wore it all the time. One day he hangs it where he usually hangs his hat up. He's on another tour. Bitter takes his hat, brings it in the kitchen, takes Ajax, and cleans out a peace symbol on it, right on the top of the circle in the hat. And he hangs it. McCormack comes back in the next day and he sees a peace symbol on his hat. He went ballistic. He went crazy trying to figure out who did this. Nobody ever 'fessed up. At the time that was the Vietnam era where the peace symbol was the anti-Christ itself.

Chief Dolak was a funny guy, too. I went to a multiple with Dolak, third alarm, factory fire Down Neck. He was the Deputy. Fire's out. We're up on the third or fourth floor overhauling. He comes walking up the stairs and he's got a roll of toilet paper and he's throwing it over all the sprinklers. Looping it over all the sprinklers. "That will screw up the Arson Squad." He did the whole third floor with this stuff, streamers. Just to see if they'd figure it out. He loved doing that kind of stuff.

Andy Marcell was on the Second Tour on Central Avenue. I was on the Third Tour, so we came in contact once a week pretty much, but he was always on. He was always on, Andy. Funny guy. He'd go around putting newspapers in everybody's boots. All kinds of silly stuff like that. He was funny. Another practical joker was Al Catalano. He'd go around squirting transmission fluid under Tommy Saccone's car all the time. He'd have Tommy half way to Aamco. He'd put little rubber duckies in Mendola's pockets in his rubber coat. He'd go to a fire, reach into his pocket, and pull out a little rubber ducky, a little pair of baby shoes.

D. Prachar: The pillow fights in the bunkroom. Stuff like that, you figure girls at pajama parties or something like that. Belmont Avenue snowball fights, climbing out of the bathroom window of Five Truck into the bathroom window of Twelve Engine to sneak up on Twelve Engine. Only to find the captain coming up the stairs and you bombing him with a snowball and almost going on charges. Stuff like that you never forget. Good times, really good times. You knew on Belmont Avenue that when the first half way decent snowball could be made it was the beginning of an attack by either side. Just the different things. How different houses do different things. That was camaraderie, bust balls, but yet sit down and break bread together. Eat dinner. You wash the dishes, I cook. That's the fire department.

Firemen are just little boys who never grew up. Prime example snowball fights and water fights. Get even. Get even with the guy who never comes in. Give me the tip, I'll stick it out the window and I'll blast him. That's the little boy in you. When you were little, Johnny hit me, so I'm going to get even with him. Well, sure as hell what goes around comes around on this job and you will get even eventually.

McDonnell: We had fun. We had fun. George Daudelin is a really comical guy. George is a very good fireman, too. Excellent fireman. We were friends, so it was good. I had somebody there that I knew and helped with the Hoot. He'd get on you. You had to take Hoot with a grain of salt, because if he knew he could get to you, boy he would bust you no end. I used to ignore him, so he used to get frustrated with me. He'd give up. "Everything I say to him, he don't pay no attention to me." He'd just give up. I really learned a lot from him. He was a great fireman. I got to work with a lot of good fireman. We had fun. My most enjoyable time on the fire department was those five years I spent as a fireman. We had some hilarious times. George and I were like a change from what they were used to because we were like crazy like they were, but we didn't drink and we didn't get in trouble. I think they put up with all the shit we did because they were happy that we didn't cause more trouble.

McGrory was the chief. I don't know how he put up with us. He would come. We would be dressed up like Soul Train one day. I remember this one Saint Patrick's Day me and George had this coat and this little green derby on. I had a big paper bow tie. George was singing "A Little Bit of Heaven." McGrory would come out the door, look, and say "Ahh". Turned around, he didn't want to see anything. He went the other way. We used to have some great times. At Christmas time we used to get the stereo and play the Christmas music out the windows. Jimmy Langenbach coming to work one day. He said it looked like one of those World War II movies with the soldiers coming and the music playing. We had a lot of fun. A lot of good times. They were wild. They were wild guys.

Ryan: I have a story with Harry Carter. We're in the same company. We had a fire on West Market Street. Oh, Jeeze, I forget what the cross street was. Anyway, it was down below. Probably Boston Street, somewhere in there. Herby Foster was the driver. Melody was our captain. Get done, knocked down, we had loaded all the hose up on the rig. Herby Foster was driving. Tommy was in the cab.

Harry and I get off, stop the traffic on West Market Street. Herby and Tommy are talking. Herby puts it in second gear and starts taking off, went back to the firehouse. Left me and Harry standing on the corner. They called back in service. We're still on West Market Street. Eddy Jankowski's in Three Truck. He comes along. "What's the matter with you two?" "Tommy Melody just left us here." "Come on with me." So, we jump on Three Truck and he takes us up to Eleven Engine and he gets a hold of Tommy. "Why'd you leave your two guys there?" "What? What? I left them there? I thought they were on the back step?" Because they backed into Central Avenue, that was a dangerous place. Always traffic. This time there was no traffic on the street, so they backed in, closed the door. About fifteen minutes later we come in with Three Truck. They never even noticed. And they had gone back in service. There wasn't anybody there.

A lot of true characters on the job. Great people. You have to get into a little bit of should we say horseplay, just to maintain your sanity with the fire load that was on you all the time. It's probably just a natural reflex to alleviate the devastation that you were up close and personal with every day. There were a lot of practical jokes, all good natured. Talk about writing a book, Tommy Melody would always say, "I could write a book about this, but nobody would believe it."

H. Carter: I was filling in for Louie Formisano in the gig as the acting Third Battalion and it was my birthday. I made rounds as the acting unknown Battalion Chief. This was in the days of the gong show in the early 1980s where the guy had the paper bag. He was the unknown comic. I took a paper bag, painted it white at the top, cut eyes out. Vinny McGraph was driving and we pulled up at all the firehouses on rounds. I would get out of the car and they would hit the bell, thinking it was the real chief. I got out with the bag over my head and introduced myself as the unknown acting Battalion Chief. Then we proceeded to go back to Fifteen Engine and played cards all night. I won about seventy-five dollars. We had a great meal. We had a ball. It's because I enjoyed all that, that I didn't study, and

I didn't make Battalion Chief years ahead of where I should have, because I was an asshole and made the mistake of loving my job.

Langenbach: It was the best time. I never had so much fun as I had with the guys at Five Truck. It was like summer camp. It was amazing. You can never recapture that interaction between all the guys in the truck, the guys in the engine, the guys on the different tours and each other. We worked opposite the second tour. And it was an ongoing battle between us and them. The second tour then was Georgie Daudelin, Tommy McDonnell, Frank Leber, who will go straight to heaven because he put up with all of us, and Richie Schmoemer. Who else was over there? I don't know. Cliff and Mike Constantino were over on the engine. Oh, Hoot Gibson, Hooter was the other one. But it was just practical joke on top of practical joke. It just never stopped.

Evaporated milk, the best glue in the world. You could stick anything to anything with evaporated milk. It's the super glue, the crazy glue of the '70s. So, there would be all kinds of pictures on everybody's refrigerator. Belmont Avenue had the reputation of having at least one refrigerator per tour. They were always locked because half the time you didn't want to know what was in there, but they were always locked. So, with that there was a battle between Hoot and Billy Quirk. That was on going. I mean it was a daily war. One of the things was to cook eggs with butter. Billy hated the smell of butter. So, when Bill worked the night Hooter would come in. The first thing he would do is take a skillet and put butter in it. Just cook the butter. And he would go over the pole hole and hold it under and go back. "You mother." is all you'd hear. They would take the evaporated milk and take an egg out of the carton and put in a little drop of evaporated milk and put the egg back in there. So, when Quirk went to get the egg, the egg broke. They would put Quirk's coffee cup up on the highest shelf and fill it with water. So, when he went to get his coffee, he'd hit himself with water. It was just an amazing place.

The seventy-two hours off was too long. You had to be back. You're just going to miss something. Something was going to happen. Half the time you didn't go home. In between your nights you'd stay around the firehouse or maybe go out and come back and have lunch with the guys and hang out or whatever. You just didn't want to leave. It was a lot of fun.

My first night in Five Truck, fourth tour relieved the first tour. The first tour had their own reputation. I got put in a garbage can, stuffed in a garbage can and carried next door to Gershenbaum's and they tried to trade me for a case of beer. I don't know if they got the beer. That's when Artie and Sidney were both there. We have a perfectly good white kid, we'll trade him for a case of beer. And I'm in the garbage can.

Funny story with DeTroia, I love telling this story. He came over to us, we had Chief Borringer for a long time. Freddy Borringer was a real nice guy, but he was straight as an arrow. When he filled out the vacation book he went from beginning to end. There's no crossing over the vacation period. You take your six days here. But I want two days and two days. No, that was not allowed. So, he was that way. Chief DeTroia was a little easier going, a little milder. Great Battalion Chief, great guy at a fire, great guy to work for, but he had his own peculiarities. He was big on the uniform and Belmont Avenue was just the antithesis of that. You put together whatever you could put together. For a while we were the Belmont slashers with the knitted hats. Charlie DeLillo never wore socks. So, anyway Chief DeTroia's big thing was he wanted to see everybody in black socks. He didn't care. You got to have black socks. I want to see black socks.

So this is going on and on and on. Bob Schimpf was our captain by then. One day it was myself, Wayne, Charlie, Pat Durkin, and Schimpfer. We decided when the chief came around making his rounds that we were going to be naked except for black socks. So we did that. We hear him on the air. We know he's making his rounds. We know the route he takes. He goes to Ten Engine, then he comes to Twelve and Five Truck, and then he goes up to the Deputy's house. So, we're sitting around the kitchen naked, nothing, just the socks on.

Artie Gershenbaum from next door, the liquor store, had a key to the firehouse. Artie comes into the kitchen to get a cup of coffee. We're all sitting around with no clothes on. He goes, "Hi, Schimpfer, Jim, Charlie, Pat. How are you guys doing?" Never says a word. Gets his cup of coffee and leaves. Poor Chief DeTroia comes in and he had Joe Racioppi as his driver. Racioppi could just about get air. I thought he was going to cough up a lung he's laughing so hard. And DeTroia goes, "All right, I don't care what you wear, but you got to wear clothes. You don't have socks on, just wear clothes." And that was it. He had only been with us for a little while. But, what a great chief, great guy.

They didn't call Twelve Engine the cage for nothing. When they were putting the addition onto Five Truck they were going to make the biggest mistake possible. They're going to make us both eat together, so they put the kitchen in the middle of the two firehouses. They were going to join us. It was like two separate worlds. Now they're going to join us together. That wasn't going to work. We knew that. That was a disaster from day one.

That kitchen is still there. There's a big table. Nobody sits at it. I think if you go there it's like the leper colony. If you're banned you go sit in the middle. But when they were building it, there was a lot going on between the two houses. We were having fun on top of fun, especially between the tours, across tours, whatever. One night we took the cement blocks and we blocked up Twelve Engine's door so they couldn't get out the back door to come across to Five Truck. We just put cinder block up, just blocked it all up and left it that way. That was the one.

Hoot Gibson was in Twelve Engine at the time and he was saving bricks. He was going to brick his house, brick the front of his house. So, he was going to foundations in the area that were left in the ground when they tore down buildings and getting loads of bricks. He would store them in his locker. When he got a locker full, then he would put them in his car and he would take them home. So, one night Jimmy and I open his locker. There's a wall of bricks. We went and made cement up. Plastered the whole thing. Plastered it solid. So, now he opens it up and it's a solid wall. And we wrote in it like, "Fuck you Hooter." Well, we didn't tell him who did it for a while, but he laughed so hard. He said that's the best anybody ever got him.

When Volkswagon came out with the Rabbit diesel, Jimmy Wiggins and Richie Schoemer were living down the shore so it made sense to them to buy one. So, they both brought one. Richie got the little pick up and Jimmy got the rabbit. Well, Anthony Crecco was on the second tour. Anthony lived in East Hanover. You could almost fall out of bed and land in the firehouse. He bought one too. Everybody started talking about the gas mileage. You're getting like fifty miles to the gallon or whatever. So, we siphoned diesel out of Five Truck's fuel tank and added to Anthony's tank, like a gallon here a gallon there. He was keeping track of his gas mileage. Now he comes in, "Oh, I'm getting fifty-five miles to the gallon. I'm getting sixty miles to the gallon. I'm getting seventy miles." "Get out of here, Anthony. You can't be." "No, no they told me after I broke it in, it would be getting more and more miles." So, we got him to like a hundred miles to the gallon. Then we start doing the opposite. We start siphoning fuel out of his car. Now his mileage starts going down. We got him down to like twenty-five miles to the gallon. "This piece of shit, I should never have bought it." Never told him about that. Never told him.

When I went over to Six Engine, we were with the Deputy. Oh, some of the things they did to his driver. They used to take him and take the rope bag and tie him in his bunk. We'd get an alarm. We got a job. The job goes to a whatever and so now Chief Maresca's got to respond so I get the, "Oh, Jim would you come up here again. Jim, tell the boys they can't tie my driver to his bunk. It took ten minutes to get him untied, Jim. Tell them they can't do that anymore." They wrapped him up in register tape instead.

The city was doing a survey. They hired a consultant to come in and do a survey. Retired Chief O'Hagan from New York comes into Six Engine and just before he gets there they had taken the chief's driver and hung him up by his belt loop on the coat rank. So, here he is hanging up in the air suspended right next to the door going out to the apparatus from the kitchen. He's hanging up there and here comes Chief Maresca. Here comes Chief O'Hagan. And there's the chief's driver hanging up there on the thing. So, O'Hagan looks up and there's the driver. No response. He's seen it before. He was from New York.

They took him one time and they locked him in the bathroom by the kitchen, the little bathroom, and then squirted lighter fluid under the door and set the lighter fluid on fire. So, here he's going, "Let me out. Let me out." By the time we open the door, he's standing on top of the toilet with soot all over him. We had a good time in that house, good bunch of people. Like I said, some of the best firemen I ever worked with, that crew there. That's what I tell everybody, I've always been blessed. As a fireman I worked with great firemen, as an officer I worked with great firemen. I've always had that blessing. Even going to the Arson Squad. I had a great bunch of guys. I know today there are a lot of problems with different guys and whatever. I never had any of that. I just must have slipped through at the right time.

Connell: I'll start with some of my escapades in Five Engine. I am known more or less as a ball buster. Here are three of my favorite incidents. The first one was Georgie Alfano, he's a prince among men. If you look at him he looks the spitting image of Lou Costello. He had nine kids so he was always working part time. He used to drive delivering pipe-fittings and stuff, real heavy pipe fittings for major industrial things, when he wasn't working in the firehouse.

He was hard of hearing and we were always pulling jokes on him. Like we'd all go upstairs, lie in bed, when George came up at night, he usually went to bed around twelve o'clock for some reason or other. But we'd wait for him to get in bed and take his hearing aids out and we'd all get up and start running down the stairs like we had a run. Poor George would get up, jump out of bed, get dressed, slide down the pole, and we'd all be back upstairs in bed. He'd be down there looking around for us. This was a common occurrence. Everybody did it to Georgie.

Another time, Captain Farrell at that time was a Boy Scout leader and they were having a paper drive. I was studying for Captain and Georgie had a 1964 Chevy station wagon. I asked Georgie if he could watch the book. At that time, the Deputy was in the house, so somebody had to be sitting by the book at all times. He thought I was going to study. He said, "Sure, go ahead. Take your time." I snuck out the back of the firehouse and I proceeded to take all the papers that the captain had accumulated for this

Boy Scout drive, take them apart, and fold up each piece of paper individually. I filled up his '64 Chevy station wagon front to back so you couldn't get another piece of paper in if you tried. This took me approximately three and a half hours.

As I went back in I thanked Georgie for watching the book. He went upstairs to bed and I finished my book watch. In the morning, about six o'clock I heard some commotion. There I found Georgie Alfano trying to squash the papers down enough so he could get in it and drive home to show his wife what the guys did to him. It took five garbage cans to empty out his station wagon.

Second incident in Five Engine is with Charlie Alaimo. It was a hot summer day. We're bored, and I threw a cup of water on him. Things started escalating. It finally ended up with me going outside and taking the garden hose we had to wash the rig with and spraying Charlie and chasing him all over the firehouse with it. Charlie got so mad at me, he ran into the kitchen sink, took his shoe off, started filling it up with water, and throwing the water at me out of his shoe.

Another incident, we were sitting in front of the firehouse, again it was during the summer. Georgie Alfano was sitting reading the newspaper about a lot of fires down south Jersey in the forest. Being a smoker, I always had matches on me or a cigarette lighter. Well, Georgie's sitting in the chair propped up against the firehouse with the paper in front of him. I lit the back page on fire. I'm looking and the flames are about three feet over the paper. Now he's so intent on the story and flames are starting to get close to his fingers now. So, I said, "George." He looked up and he saw the paper. Newspapers went flying all over Congress Street on fire.

One more time with Charlie Alaimo, I had a '74 Honda. It was a great car. It ran great mechanically, but the whole body was rusting out. The hinge rusted through the body door on the driver's side. So, every time you opened the door up it would like fall down. You would have to pick it up to close it. You'd close it three or four times to get it to close. One day Charlie was laying down taking a nap in the kitchen area. We had a couch there. Teddy Hartman was down from Two Truck. He had firecrackers and he told me I didn't have a hair on my ass if I didn't throw a firecracker in and wake Charlie up. So, being macho, I tried to show him I'm not ball-less and hairless, I did throw a firecracker in, which seemed to piss Charlie off. He went outside. He knew I had a problem with the door and he ripped the door open and he put a big dent in it. The whole thing was, a month and a half later I sold Charlie the car for four hundred dollars. So, he had this broken door now that he broke.

High Street was a challenge. In Five Engine basically, there's nobody to bust my balls back, so I felt quite confident in myself because I had nobody to repay the favors. When I went to High Street I found out I was not as good as I thought I was with ball busting and if you busted somebody's balls, you usually got your balls busted back. It was a never-ending syndrome. Once you started, it never stopped. We've done everything from cans of water on doors that fell on you, beds turned upside down with the mattress on them so when you sat on them they just fall apart. Ropes being tied to your bed while you'd be sleeping. All of the sudden your bed would be sliding across the bunkroom. Everybody would be downstairs pulling a rope through the pole hole and you'd be flying across the bunkroom floor.

We also didn't confine our ball busting to people working in the firehouse. Turned out anybody in the neighborhood was fair game. We had the roof, which was a flat roof, three story building. There have been times we were up there shooting bottle rockets off at passing pedestrians.

Another time the fire department issued us these little plastic green fluorescent things. If you got in trouble, you're supposed to take it out of your pocket, break it and it's a night glow light. It's supposed to last you so many hours. About five o'clock one morning the garbage trucks were coming and loading the garbage up. It was a hot night and nobody was sleeping much that night. Anyway, one of the guys gets the bright idea; let's have some fun with the garbage men. So, it's two of us sitting out in the front smoking, me and Freddy Paskas. One of the guys went up to the roof and he took one of these breaking plastic sticks that glowed green and he threw it off the roof. Me and Freddy put on an act. "Oh, look at what fell out of the sky." Look at this. Look at that. And the garbage men were looking at it. They couldn't believe what they were seeing. "Oh, it must be a meteorite or something." So, Freddy picked it up. "Oh, let me get rid of this." So he takes it down the alleyway. Brings it to the garbage can in the back and he cuts it open and he puts the green stuff on his hands and his face. He comes out all fluorescent now. He goes, "I hope that stuff wasn't radioactive." The two garbage men jumped in the truck. I don't think we ever saw them again. Like I said, when you hit High Street you hit the pros. They didn't get much better than that. We went through a little bit of everything up there.

Pignato: My best person at Eleven Engine was Andy Marcell. If it weren't for him I probably would have hated this job so much. He made me see what humor was on this job. Andy Marcell was the guy. Somebody had given me five gallons of latex. That's what you use to make a mold. You make a mold and pour plaster in it. You can make a mold of anything that stays still. Well, I had this big old candle thing my wife got from a ceramics fire. One side was a monk the other side was a big penis. This was about a foot and a half long and I had a smaller one. So we were in there and we're going to make a mold of this. I'm putting twenty coats of latex on there. After it cures you peel it off. Now you have a mold. We had a big mold and a small mold. Well the small mold was just right. It looked like the size of an ice pop. Andy gets a bunch of ice cream sticks from his son and puts them aside. He uses all different colors of Jell-O to make cocksicles. Cocksicles. He kept them in the freezer. Every time someone came in there he'd play a joke on them. So one time they went to the Academy. Chief Wall was still in residence there. He had all these big shots from all over the country because they're starting up the National Fire Academy.

Marcell's there and everybody's laughing because he has a whole tray full of these cocksicles with a cover over them so they won't melt. The Chief says "What do you have there?" He says "I don't want to show you Chief. You'll get mad." " No, come on what do you have?" So he's showing it. All these guys from all over the country are looking at these cocksicles. Hey, these are cute. "Say, Andy. What do you use for a mold." "I can't tell you Chief." "Come on Andy, you can tell us. We're all firemen." "No, Chief you'll get mad if I tell you." "I won't get mad." "You sure, Chief?" "I won't get mad Andy. Tell us. What did you use for a mold?" "Well, Chief, we used your helmet." "My helmet?" That was it. Eleven Engine was banned from going down there.

He used to plug poor Captain Haran. When Captain Haran would be upstairs studying on his bed, Andy actually took a ladder, put it up on the window sill, went up there, and set there staring at him. Until he looked up, saw Andy's face at the window, and jumped out of his skin. Andy says, "I love you." He was constantly playing Captain Haran.

Another time he got me. The stairway on Eleven Truck went alongside the building. There was a window halfway up. You can go out onto a little roof out there. It was the middle of a snow storm. I was working for somebody on the second tour. So he says "We're going to play a joke on Captain Haran." So, I say, "Okay." I'm game for anything. "Go out the window. When Eddy Haran comes down the stairs, I'll keep him busy, you just reach out and grab him. We'll scare him." "Okay." I go out there. It's snowing like hell. I had about six inches of snow on me. I mean, it was actually built up. Eddy Haran comes down the stairs, looks out the window, I'm standing on this little roof with two or three inches of snow on me. I'm not moving. I have nothing but a light shirt on. He just looked at me, shook his head and walked away. He never talked with me again after that. I looked like I was something from outer space.

I got even with Andy one time. Someone was always trying to get even with him. Now trying to get him on anything was hard. He's so quick. I got in about five-thirty in the morning one time, crawled into his locker. He used to be the first guy up, make coffee for everybody. So, I got in his locker and I put a ski mask on. I'm down there. He started to shave. It's six o'clock in the morning. He comes to his locker. He's a tall guy. I just parted the clothes, so you see my face. I just reached out and went "Ah." He screamed. I felt so bad. Woke everybody up. I can't get out of the locker. Big Al Alfano did the same thing to him. Climbed into his bed, Andy got up to go to the bathroom in the middle of the night, comes back, and pulls back his covers. There's Al in his bed.

You hear some of the stories about his war record. He was quite a soldier. He saved a lot of stuff in Korea. It's amazing. He's such a genius.

Perdon: Ball busting was huge, huge, huge. You were on the giving end. You were on the receiving end, no matter what. No matter who you were. Some guys yes, you were on the receiving more often and a lot more, but you always managed. You would get even. You would come back every once in a while and everybody was hoping.

I remember one time they used to have that huge, big cock. I was on the book and I said something to Cody. I pissed him off. Next thing I know I walk out of the watch room and hanging from the pole hole is this big cock.

We were doing things to the chief's driver, but he thought we loved him every time we did it. "Oh, they love me. That's why they bust my balls." Pretty much everything was pretty verbal. We would do some crazy things like tie him up to the bed post. Lie him down on the bed. Put all the pieces of furniture on him and things like that. They were just funny incidents, funny little things like Birdman walking around on the top of the lockers. He's straddling one locker, from one locker to the other locker over the chief's door. And all of the sudden here comes the chief out of the room. Birdman's up there in his underwear. The chief never looked up. Walks out to the bathroom, comes back in. Birdman is still up there.

Ricca: Ball busting, I'd have to say the greatest ball busting I've ever seen was in Five Truck. What I heard my brother Joe used to do in that kitchen was great. There was a ceiling fan and he would put flour on top of the ceiling fan. Hoot Gibson would come in in the morning and flip the switch. And Quirk used to scream at my brother because my brother is nocturnal. Joe was up all night. Quirk would yell at him, "Will you get a pair of God damn slippers." But Joe did stuff like tie a milk bottle or a soda bottle on a string, lower it down and knock on the door with it and then raise it up. The book man would come out and look around. He would do the same thing again. He had a knack for writing on the ticker-tape just at the right spots. When the box would come in, he put down, "You're going to miss this one Quirk."

Ray Frost was deathly afraid of rats, mice. He'd run into a burning building without a thought, but he didn't like mice. They found a rat one day, dead, tied a knot in its tail; tied it to his locker on the coat rack part, the coat pole. That didn't go over too great. Then one day they must have caught about ten mice and put them in the coffee can. So, I came in first and I go to open the can, but I said, "These guys always clean the kitchen and make coffee. Something's up." And I put my hand on the lid and "tip, tip." I look in. There're the mice jumping up. Well, Ray walks in. He opens it up and it was like a carnival snake coming out of that thing. He screamed. He jumped up on the bench. It was nuts.

And of course the old, put a hole in the soda can or whatever beverage you were drinking, so when you drank it, it would spill all over you. The old air compressors had a relief pin and guys would tie off to that, send the sting upstairs and about three in the morning when the book man was sleeping, yank the pin. And the thing would sound like a bomb going off. That would wake you up kind of abruptly. Nailing people's shoes to the wall. But probably some of the best meals and best jokes I've ever had were in the firehouse.

Gesualdo: Oh, I love the ball busting in the firehouse. It's the best part of the job. Having a reputation for being a buster, you appreciate that. It always seemed to be an unwritten rule. You say whatever you want to anybody, just don't put your hands on him. I remember a few times where people made the mistake of putting their hands on somebody.

But as far as the busting part, some houses have different rules and you have to kind of know the rules when you go into that particular station or firehouse; where their guidelines are. Some will include family members and things like that in their busting or criticism. Other houses, like here, we kind of just keep it to each other. You don't get involved with family in discussing sexual things and preferences and things like that. So we always seem to have a little kind of a barrier around certain issues and topics. Whereas other firehouses, you walk in and their talking about people's mothers and daughters, so you have to understand where you are and let them know, somehow that you don't discuss things like that. But I think it all works out. I think firemen are some of the cleverest individuals, I mean with spontaneous comments and remarks. They'd probably make the best standup comics if they ever wanted to have a part-time job. I always thought that.

List of Interviewees

Baldino, Captain Barney, letter to the author 20 September, 2002. (appointed 1951)

Belzger, Firefighter William, 4 October, 2004, transcript. (appointed 1959)

Bisogna, Captain Joseph, 25 July, 2001, transcript. (appointed 1974)

Butler, Captain James, 3 September 1993, transcript. (appointed 1963)

Cahill, Firefighter Joseph, 25 June 1991, transcript. (appointed 1963)

Carragher, Deputy Chief William, November 1994, transcript. (appointed 1960)

Carter, Battalion Chief Harry, 12 June, 1991, transcript. (appointed 1973)

Charpentier, Firefighter Frederick, 22 August 1993, transcript. (appointed 1959)

Cody, Battalion Chief James, 26 October 1999, transcript. (appointed 1964)

Connell, Battalion Chief Anthony, 26 February, 1999, 24 November, 2003. (appointed 1974)

Cosby, Firefighter Joseph, 22 August, 1991, transcript. (appointed 1969)

Denvir, Captain John, 13 September 1993, transcript. (appointed 1959)

Deutch, Firefighter Charles, 14 November 1993, transcript. (appointed 1953)

Dunn, Deputy Chief Edward, 14 August1991, 29 August 1997, transcript. (appointed 1959)

Finucan, Deputy Chief James, 7 August 1991, transcript. (appointed 1969)

Freda, Deputy Chief Alfred, 12, 25, 26 July 1991, transcript. (appointed 1959)

Fredette, Firefighter Reggie, 3 November, 1993, transcript. (appointed 1942)

Freeman, Captain Richard, 20, 21 August 1991, transcript. (appointed 1956)

Garrity, Battalion Chief Joseph, May 1992, transcript. (appointed 1964)

Gesualdo, Captain Al, 21 July, 2003, transcript. (appointed 1978)

Grehl, Deputy Chief Frederick, 7 August 1993, transcript. (appointed 1948)

Grehl, Captain Thomas, 29 May, 2002, transcript. (appointed 1971)

Griffith, Chief Fire Alarm Operator Robert, 3 July, 1991, transcript. (appointed 1953)

Haran, Captain Edward, 5 February 2001, transcript. (appointed 1961)

Harris, Captain William, 13 December 1999, transcript. (appointed 1961)

Highsmith, Firefighter Gerald, 2 June 1994, transcript. (appointed 1963)

Kinnear, Deputy Chief David, 28 September 1992, transcript. (appointed 1947)

Knight, Firefighter Gerald, 19 June 1991, transcript. (appointed 1964)

Langenbach, Deputy Chief James, 24 October, 2002, transcript. (appointed 1973)

Langevin, Firefighter Robert, 23 February, 1999, transcript. (appointed 1974)

Luxton, Captain Charles, 14 January, 1999, transcript. (appointed 1973)

Marcell, Firefighter Andrew, 23 September 1998, transcript. (appointed 1959)

Masters, Firefighter Anthony, 24 March, 2004, transcript. (appointed 1947)

Masterson, Captain Andrew, 6 April, 2005, transcript. (appointed 1949)

McCormack, Sr. Deputy Chief James, 14 June 1991, transcript. (appointed 1949)

McDonnell, Captain Thomas, 30 March, 1999, 16 April, 1999, transcript. (appointed 1970)

McGee, Captain Raymond, 26 October 2000, transcript. (appointed 1956)

McGovern, Battalion Chief Thomas, 8 June, 2001, transcript. (appointed 1968)

McGrory. Deputy Chief Albert, 31 August 1991, transcript. (appointed 1957)

Melodick, Firefighter William, June, 2001, transcript. (appointed 1970)

Miller, Battalion Chief Joseph, 16, 21 August 1991, transcript. (appointed 1959)

Perdon, Captain George, 9 June, 2003, transcript. (appointed 1974)

Pianka, Firefighter George, 15 June, 2001, transcript. (appointed 1970)

Pignato, Captain Nicholas, 26 May, 1999, transcript. (appointed 1974)

Prachar, Captain Daniel, 12 August, 1991, transcript. (appointed 1968)

Redden, Fire Chief Joseph, 16 September 2002, transcript. (appointed 1947)

Ricca, Battalion Chief Ronald, 1 June, 2000, transcript. (appointed 1974)

Rotonda, Firefighter Gerard, 3 May, 2000, transcript. (appointed 1970)

Ryan, Battalion Chief Joseph, 28 September, 1999, transcript. (appointed 1973)

Smith, Firefighter James, 2 September 1998, transcript. (appointed 1959)

Stoffers, Battalion Chief Carl, 2 September 1998, transcript. (appointed 1956)

Vesey, Firefighter Edward, 15 June 1999, transcript. (appointed 1948)

Vetrini, Captain Joseph, 14 September, 1993, transcript. (appointed 1946)

Wall, Deputy Chief Edward, 13 September, 2000, transcript. (appointed 1954)

Wargo, Captain Andrew, 6 June 1991, transcript. (appointed 1964)

www.ingramcontent.com/pod-product-compliance
Lightning Source LLC
Chambersburg PA
CBHW031839090426
42741CB00005B/290

* 9 7 8 1 9 7 0 0 3 4 1 6 5 *